the BOOK
of YOU

the BOOK of YOU

Discover
God's Plan and
Transform
Your Future

TERRELL FLETCHER

Waterfall
PRESS

Published by Grand Harbor Press, Grand Haven, MI

www.brilliancepublishing.com

Amazon, the Amazon logo, and Grand Harbor Press are trademarks of Amazon.com, Inc., or its affiliates.

ISBN-13: 9781503935754
ISBN-10: 1503935752

Cover design by Jeff Miller, Faceout Studio

Printed in the United States of America

AUTHOR'S NOTE

The stories in this book were composed from memory without additional research and some of the names and identities of the people have been altered to protect privacy.

TABLE OF CONTENTS

Introduction: Your Creator's Intent

"If your daily life seems poor, do not blame it; blame yourself that you are not poet enough to call forth its riches; for the Creator, there is no poverty."

—Rainer Maria Rilke

I know how intimidating it can be to adopt a whole new outlook on life—I've done it. There was scarcely a season in my life more uncertain than when I was forced to turn my back on my old world, the world of professional football. And, perhaps in moments of raw honesty, I will admit that it was football that turned its back on me—the game simply no longer needed me. What a reality. For the first time in my life, I felt age and attrition catch up with me. I was obligated to retire from the game I loved.

After eight years with the San Diego Chargers, my greatest challenge to date was deciding to face the new realities of my future. The fear, uncertainty, and ambiguity of what the next season of my life held was real and tangible, and to say I was confused would be an understatement. For over fifteen years, I'd lived as a footballer. It dictated my schedule, educational pursuits, personal economics, friends, business decisions, associates, ideals, and even what foods I chose to eat. Not one sector of my life could have been substantially altered without considering football, because whether consciously or subconsciously, above all, I showed up in this world as "Terrell Fletcher, Professional Football Player." I wasn't just leaving a game; I was leaving an identity.

Much like the empty nester whose last child has left the house, an employee whose factory has just closed down, a new divorcée, or a person who is simply unfulfilled—I was searching to answer a question deeper than: What would I *do* next? I was searching to answer: Who would I *be* next? I felt lost, disoriented, and directionless. So there I was, in a stare down with my future.

I never wanted to be one of those aging athletes who hangs on for years after it's clear that he no longer "has it," signing desperate one-year contracts and moving from team to team because he can't let go. Neither did I want to be one of those guys who hangs around the football crowds, hoping that someone will remember him and comment on the "glory years" and yesterday's accomplishments so that he can feel like he still has present worth.

Though months had passed since I'd left the football world, I remained severely perplexed. I sensed there was more to my personal meaning than any one set of actions I could perform (or in this case, no longer perform). I just needed to find out what that was. In order to do that, however, I needed to let go of the game and make a clean break toward something new. My reality was that I was no longer a footballer, and I needed more than another job; I needed to find my personal and fundamental reason for being on this Earth. I was acutely aware that I did not want to ever go through the emotions of feeling unnecessary again, and I needed to find a purpose that could not be taken away by age, ability, or an employer. I needed to become acquainted with the underpinnings for all that I have ever done and would ever do moving forward, and contribute to this life in a way and with a clarity that I did not have before. I needed to discover my true purpose and meaning—I was about to embark on one of my biggest journeys of transition.

Transitions are about a lot more than the change itself; they are about understanding the life span of seasons and the powerful role that life purpose plays in bringing true significance and meaning to every season you enter and exit. It requires courage to take this journey through the seasons of your life because, as certain as they begin, they also come to an end, and often without our consent or readiness. So it takes courage to face the possibilities of a future that, though uncertain, may very well contain a vibrant, dominating, renewed purpose and meaning. It can be a little frightening to see yourself doing something new with such a ferocious passion, leaving what you were doing behind. But can you imagine a better way to live, and serve humanity and God, than with ferocious passion?

To do that I realized that I would need to walk with intention, in an intention that was higher than my own—I needed to discover and walk in God's intention for my life. I soon realized that seeking this higher intention not only changed how I related to the world around me but changed the way the world related to me. Realizing God's intention for my life has allowed me to make radical choices that transformed my physical and psychological location. My personal desires, my lifestyle, shifted, and even some of my social circles did as well.

It can be terrifying to make decisions that you know will turn you away from certain opportunities and, sometimes, the people who have been your support and strength, but it may be necessary. Once you discover your *Creator's Intent*, you will be guided by Divine programming and a spiritual mapping that yields results that are of Divine proportion; you will experience true meaning and significance, an abiding happiness and joy, and the sense that you are partnering with the Divine to bring

His will forward on Earth. And what I discovered is that the Creator's Intent was remarkably closer to me than I once believed.

My move to ministry was not just a job change but a destiny discovery. The stigma of being a minister is so powerful that it was a shock to many people in my life, especially people who were accustomed to me living the privileged life of a professional athlete. Some people grew uncomfortable around me. Invitations to social events decreased. I was excluded from certain conversations and activities that I previously would have been the first to be informed of. Endorsements and job opportunities for which I would have been a shoo-in were not even offered. My new direction was sincere, but it came with a high cost.

But it wasn't as though I wasn't warned. A well-intentioned advisor at the time told me very clearly about the potential backlash of being so public about my faith and becoming a minister. He did not want me to denounce my faith but only to not wear it so publicly initially. To that I responded, "My new employer is God, and He sees everything. How do you suppose I can get away with not endorsing the company product?" The reality of my new direction had such a disruptive impact that it didn't just affect me—it affected my family, friends, and business associates. Some of them were unsure about how to approach me because, in their eyes, I was becoming unrecognizable—a new type of person.

In reality I was not; they were just unable to see how two separate industries, football and the ministry, could so perfectly weave together in the singular purpose that resided in me. What they witnessed was a progressive transformation from my former activities to one that more clearly represented my deeper Creator's Intent. I was operating and expressing the virtues I was always meant to express, allowing me to be defined by who I truly am and not merely according to tasks I could perform. This is what happens when a person aligns themselves with the Creator's Intent: he becomes a transformed person.

What Is a Creator's Intent?

To answer that, I will use a logically truthful statement about bicycles: they don't assemble themselves. Nor do meals cook themselves or paintings paint themselves. It doesn't matter if the product of the creation is a bicycle, a four-course meal, a painting, or an entire cosmos—everything begins with a "creative concept" in the mind of a creator. Having a creator with a concept ensures that whatever created will have purpose and possibility, an intended function and intended results. These intended functions and results are the Creator's Intent:

> *God's conceptual purpose and possibility for your life that includes your highest intended functions that ensure accompanying results.*

The *intent* is the objective of the creation. It's what the creation is *for*, what it should be performing and accomplishing. Most important, the Creator's Intent is the "why" of what's created. If we're wondering why something works as it does, or doesn't work as it should, we can usually trace those answers back to the creator's vision.

Our Creator had intent in mind when He fashioned us from His visions. The Creator had an idea in mind for what you would do, who you would become, and how you would impact the world around you. Think of that intent, that fundamental design, as your original "programming." Whatever function the Creator had in mind for you, that's your highest purpose. Discovering, pursuing, and performing that purpose is what you were meant to do with your life.

We all crave answers to the deepest questions of our hearts: How can we find significance in our lives? What contributions can we make to this world? How can we experience genuine joy, peace, and fulfillment? The Creator is the source of all of those answers, and He has an intention for all that He created, and that includes you:

The Creator had (and has) a specific, purposeful intention for how you should be using your life and your gifts.

Since God is our Creator and we are His creation, it is possible to learn many things about yourself through a relationship with Him. Even if you don't believe in a Creator, there are identifiable parts of you that provide glimpses into His "intelligent intentions" concerning you. There is a great promise from Scripture in Jeremiah 29:11 that blesses me every time I broach this topic and will be used quite a bit in different variations. It's God's admonishment to us about our existence: "I know the thoughts I think toward you, says the Lord, thoughts of peace and not of evil, to give you a future and a hope."

This verse likens God to any responsible creator: He has pondered and considered His creation's purpose—He thought about us. He is certain of this purpose. God already knows, and has always known, what you were meant to do and who you were meant to be. Though He thought about us, the trick part is, God initially holds his intentions a mystery from us because concealment entices intimacy. We tend to want to discover what is withheld from us. In the process of discovering that purpose, intimacy and a relationship with our Creator are developed, and our knowledge of the power of self and of God are examined, experienced, and proven. That also means that your goal is a simple yet vital one:

If you are to know it, you must pursue the Creator's Intent and live according to it.

SIGNIFICANCE AND SELF-WORTH

As you discover the Creator's Intent you will also discover significance and authentic self-worth. The two go hand in hand. "Significance" means that you have found a meaningful reason for being—something all of us thirst for. Also, along with knowing *that* we matter, we also long to know *where* we matter, where our contributions can make the greatest difference in the scope of humanity. God made you significant, but it is a part of your responsibility to find out in what sphere you can share that significance. When you discover that you matter and where you matter, the reward is community, respect, happiness, and a sense of wholeness.

"Self-worth" means that you are aware and acknowledge your own value and importance to this world. The word "worth" implies a comparison; you can't determine what something is worth until you compare it to something else. Years ago, when I was selling my house, the realtor had to determine the value of the homes similar to mine before she could determine the worth of my home. Those "comps" helped determine the value of my home. It's the same with you and your self-worth, except that when you compare yourself truly and honestly to other people, you'll discover that there is no one quite like you. You have no comps. You are unique, and God made you that way, with an individual purpose based on His intent.

God's intent for your life is so genuine and specific to you that no one else has the same features, potential, or assignment as you. God has made you rare and incomparable. And rare and incomparable objects have a high market worth! This book will help you view yourself in a new way, through the frame of His unique intent, so that you see yourself just as you are right now in this moment: worthy, capable, and expected to make a significant contribution to your family, community, and this world.

LEARN TO READ THE SIGNS

The discovery of God's intent and purpose for your life will not come through osmosis. Neither can you expect to see a nonstop burning bush as Moses did. You will have to participate in the discovery process. Purpose and significance are *revealed*, not given. God did not write your purpose in a book or tell it to your best friend to hand over when you're ready. Instead, it is in His mind and in your heart. Ecclesiastes 3:11 says, "Also he has put eternity in their hearts . . ." The Creator's Intent for you has been systematically unfolding and showing itself throughout your life. It's like a trail of bread crumbs that God wants you to follow in order to find your way to His intent. What are those bread crumbs? Here are some examples:

- Yearnings you cannot quell or readily define but you know exist
- Burdens you feel and bear
- Passions and obsessions that you can't account for
- Reoccurring social positioning
- Consistent coincidences and synchronicities
- The common things that bring you inexplicable peace, energy, or focus

These desires are given by God and are not to be confused with "wants"; the things you want can be influenced by your life experiences and may or may not match God's intent for your life. However, your yearnings—the burning desire about who you want to become and how you want your life to play out—were implanted in you before you were born.

Psalms 37:4 says, "Delight yourself also in the Lord, and He shall give you the desires of your heart." You may be familiar with this Psalm, but I want to define "delight" and "desire" to help our understanding.

Two Hebrew words for "delight" are *hepes* and *anag*. They literally mean to "bend toward" and "to be soft and pliable." I believe that to delight hints toward the joy and contentment associated with allowing oneself to be led in a certain direction, in this case toward the ideas of God our Creator. It can be said that we are to be "bent toward" God and "be soft and pliable" to His will for our life. The result is that we would then receive "the desires of our heart."

A Hebrew word for "desire" is *mish'alah*. It means "to ask or request something," such as a question a highly curious student might ask a teacher concerning a particular subject matter. To desire is to yearn for an answer. Different from your mind, where language and images of thoughts bring a certain clarity to what you are thinking, the heart operates with inner promptings and instigations. These promptings beg to be revealed, explained, and acted upon. The promise from your Creator is that, as you search and become compliant to His design for your life, He will reveal and answer the questions your heart truly yearns to ask. Like a mystery waiting to be revealed, so is the Creator's Intent for you!

This Psalm is encouraging you to choose, search, and bend yourself toward the Creator—find the part of the Divine that resides in you and align your will with His. After all, you are God's child and part of His divinity exists in you. That is your purpose. That is why, when you operate with that purpose, everything feels right. Everything comes together. Everything flows. You feel mighty and unstoppable! It doesn't prevent adversity from coming, but it situates you in your most powerful position to face and overcome it.

Discovering the Creator's Intent is like having a "good" heart attack. Many people have said that having a major health concern, like a heart attack, refocused them on their priorities and the meaning of their lives in a way nothing else ever had. Being challenged to find the Creator's Intent is like having a heart attack without actually having one. It's a shock, a wake-up call that we sometimes need to remember the value of life and get ourselves back on track.

You will have to quiet yourself and listen. You will have to take an honest look at yourself and weave the threads of your life together to make something beautiful. The raw material is in you. You just need the instructions. Your Creator has been speaking to you your entire life, and now is the time to learn to listen and discover your Creator's Intent.

The real quest in life is not to gain more material things but to find one's truest self—to one day be able to say, with certainty, "I've found me and this is who I am." Discovering God's intent for your life is the pathway to finding the *you* that you've been waiting to meet.

How to Use This Book

I find that the problem most people have with books about spirituality and personal growth is that there is no corresponding action to follow the teachings; they are philosophical and overly conceptual but not very practical. I don't want this book to be another that you read, grab a few good quotes from, and throw on a shelf, never to be looked at again. So this book takes an autobiographical approach, using stories from my journey, which help illustrate deeper truths concerning your life and God's intentions and reveal how I've walked this journey (and still am every day). It includes my own experience of exploring, practicing, learning, and honing these spiritual principles in my life as well as in the lives of those I work with. Therefore, the teachings of this book are meant to be applied if they are to bring meaning and results. Information without action renders the information far less powerful.

My goal is for this book to be a tool kit and guide you can take along your entire life journey of self-discovery. This book is about making the choice to learn, see, and explore your Creator's Intent for your life. It is your next step to create a life full of meaning and purpose—to live fully congruent with the Creator's Intent and maximize your time on Earth. Another important element of this book, which I believe is an essential reason for why I wrote it, is the *necessity* of discovering our Creator's Intent. It's the very essence of our purpose here on Earth, our true job as spiritual beings, to discover who we are and why we are here as designed by God.

You will see that your purpose and functionality will be best evident when you recognize God's intention for your life. It determines the direction you should move in, the environment you will function best in, and the causes you will most benefit. You wouldn't attempt to watch a bicycle like a television, would you? Of course not; its functionality clearly suggests that its purpose is something different. Your functionality—how you live your life from day to day—can clearly communicate God's intent in your creation. This is the book's mission.

God knows His intent for you. But this is also information you should know about yourself. God's desire is not to hide this from you but for you to be as certain about it as He is. This is why you must intentionally discover it, because discovery produces certainty. God knows that when you understand His intent, you will operate optimally and enjoy life more fully. As you move through this book, you will discover the many ways to see and understand the clues and signs God has placed in your sphere, and how to unravel the mystery.

To help you uncover your Creator's Intent, *The Book of You* is organized into nine chapters, each one focusing on specific spiritual principles. The chapters naturally build on one another, like a journey that progresses each step of the way. I recommend you experience the book chronologically initially, and bring along a journal in which to write your thoughts and insights. Each chapter concludes with reflection questions and exercises that will help you actively engage and look for the Creator's clues. Of course, if you see a chapter title that resonates with you, then feel free to follow your instincts and feelings and read it first—there could be a reason why it's calling out to you. And then, you can always come back to the other chapters, each having something unique to offer, because I do ultimately recommend that this journey be experienced as a complete journey.

One early hint: the journey to self-discovery may include some surprises. I'll say it now that you may encounter some rough patches along the way; it's not a quick and easy process. Discovering the Creator's Intent for your life involves deep self-work, and the commitment and faith you put into it will bring its rewards—rewards that will truly feed your soul. Take your time along the way; take a pause to breathe or pray for courage and the focus to pay attention to the present moment. And lastly, as to whom you pray to, whether you call this transcendent source God, as I do, or another spiritual name, I invite any and all beliefs. We are all welcome to discover who we are.

CHAPTER 1: CHOOSE TRANSFORMATION VERSUS CHANGE

"The way of the Creative works through change and transformation, so that each thing receives its true nature and destiny and comes into permanent accord with the Great Harmony: This is what furthers and what perseveres."

—Alexander Pope

The first time I renovated my house was by accident. All I initially wanted was a little more space in the living room. So I called an interior decorator to help me evaluate and manage my need. Excited at the opportunity to help, she assessed the situation and called it a "simple task." With the reasonable budget I provided, she proceeded to purchase shelving to use wall space to help get things off the floor; she bought smaller, multiuse furniture to consolidate the pieces; she arranged the configuration to allot for more walking lanes; and she painted the walls a color that was said to make a room "appear bigger."

When she finished, I had a beautiful newly colored and decorated room that indeed appeared to have more space. I was happy, initially.

However, after a few months of having to lie awkwardly on the shorter couches and squeeze into uncomfortable chairs that were perfect for the room but too small for my frame, I realized that the changes I made were not meeting my expectations. The reality was that I never really wanted the room to just appear bigger; I wanted it to actually *be* bigger. I realized that calling a decorator hadn't been the solution to my problem, so I called my contractor buddy and asked him to assess the situation.

He suggested that the only real solution to meeting my expectation was to take out the counter and make the fireplace smaller. I balked at the idea because it seemed so intrusive. When I told my buddy how I felt about the situation, his response was: "Well, you can keep moving furniture or you can solve your problem. Suit yourself." So I started the renovation project because this time I wanted to solve the problem. It was dusty and loud, and it affected other areas of the house; plus, moving the fireplace caused me to remodel the floors because of the patches that remained after the extraction. It was such an unwelcome inconvenience! But I figured that, since I had to put in a new floor, I might as well repaint the wall color that the designer had suggested to make the room "appear bigger." As inconvenient as it was, these major adjustments did the trick. It fixed the problem, finally giving me the extra space and flexibility I'd envisioned.

Life is a lot like my home remodel project. When areas of your life can no longer serve your needs or desires, you have three choices:

1. Do nothing
2. Change
3. Transform

Since you have this book in your hand, its obvious that you have chosen to forgo number one as an option, so the other two options that remain are "change" or "transform." Neither of these are bad choices, but they are quite different. Change is about adjustments (moving furniture, painting the walls), while transforming is about rebuilding (removing standing counters, rebuilding the fireplace). You will have to decide which of these you want to do as you move into determining the Creator's Intent for your life.

I knew for about a year and a half before I retired from the National Football League (NFL) that it was time for me to leave and do something new. Why? Because after over fifteen years of waking up every day excited about facing everything involved with the game—training camps, the physical bumps and bruises, the grind of learning play, surgeries and such—I noticed that my passion was waning, and it wasn't because I just needed a break.

I began to see my career as an athlete as one that no longer gave me the opportunity to satisfy my inner thirsts. Sure, playing was still fun, but the *purpose* had gone out of it, and for some reason I began to thirst for purpose over just having fun. When I was finally "released" from the San Diego Chargers (a fancy way of saying I got cut) in 2002, my initial instinct was to accept a tryout invitation from another team—and I did, with the Tampa Bay Buccaneers. As I entered the locker room and began dressing for my workout, I began to get a similar feeling in my gut about what I was doing. The more they prodded, poked, stretched, and measured every part of my body, the less inspired I became.

During my workout, I met some great coaches and potential new teammates, but I noticed a striking difference between them and me— my fire about the game was not as ablaze as theirs was. Even though I was now in Tampa Bay, the same feelings of emptiness I experienced in San Diego were still with me. On the plane home, pondering my feelings, I realized that doing the same thing in a different environment was not my answer. To do so would be a change in my life, but I needed to transform my life. My season as a pro-athlete had expired, and it was my responsibility to discover my meaning for the next season of my life;

it was mine and no one else's. Instead of feeling rejected by football, I chose to feel accepted by what was calling me into my next season, even though it felt scary. Making the Tampa Bay Buccaneers team would have been a surface change, more of the same. What I needed was something deeper, transformational.

At first, I figured that the only thing I was losing was a job, and to refill the void I just needed another one. In taking other jobs, I realized I was wrong! I was so lost. I have often described that season of life as if someone had blindfolded me and taken me a hundred miles out to sea, then left me on a raft with just a single paddle to find my way home. I was lost and did not know what to do to begin my journey home. I sorely underestimated how football had affected my life. It had become much more than an occupation; it had become my identity. It was the part of me that led the conversation when I walked into a room. I found a lot of security and significance in the title and social position of Professional Football Player. It was so embedded in everyone's psyche, mine included, that in order to renew my life, I needed more than a job change—I needed a life renovation!

I wanted more: more out of my life, my gifts, and my untapped potential. The football gridiron was no longer the soil where these seeds could take root. All of a sudden, I needed to explore the other parts of me that had the capacity to produce something more meaningful than yards and touchdowns. I was hungry for something radical—true transformation.

For a year and a half, I wrestled between the stability of pro-football and the call to do something different. What an uncomfortable feeling that was! I tried many things along the journey just because I was capable of doing them. I partnered in businesses (even starting two of my own), traveled, did sports commentating, etc., searching for what could satisfy me. The journey was messy, and though my movements were sporadic, I could tell that a transformation was already occurring within me. It was merely a matter of time before I could grasp it and began to express it outwardly.

I did not realize that bringing transformation into your life creates profound ripple effects, influencing all of the decisions you will make now and in the future: where you want to live, what you do for a living, who you want to be with, and so on. Transformation comes with a cost, and that cost is the abandonment or loss of part of your old self. This doesn't come without pain. But it's essential. In the act of transforming yourself, you will not see your world as you once did. You may not have as much in common with some of the people who used to be the center of your life. You may see that some of them are antithetical to your newly revealed direction. You might not care about the same things you once cared about. Transformation often brings a new kind of clarity about what's really important to you, and that clarity comes from God. It's important to pay attention to it.

However, God never empties your life of one thing without refilling it with something else. As you undergo your transformative process, you will find new connections and joy with new people and an environment that will help produce the outcomes you have always desired. Losses allow us to empty out what is not bringing us closer to the Creator's Intent, leaving room for God to fill us back up with what brings us meaning and purpose.

CHANGE VERSUS TRANSFORMATION

Human beings really don't like change. We get into a comfortable groove, and even if things are not that great, we will resist the urge to make wholesale changes to how we live. We'll say, "I just need to change a few things in my life and I will be back on track." But it's the track that's the problem! The idea of getting back on track suggests that by making just a few cosmetic changes in how you live, you can completely change your life in accordance with the Creator's Intent. Sadly, that's just not true.

In order to reposition your life, you probably need to make more than just a small modification to the way you've been doing things. Long-lasting results demand radical renovations. If you've been focusing your energies on making incremental "tweaks" to how you eat, pray, or speak to others, you've been concentrating on *change*, when what's really needed to align with the Creator's Intent is *transformation*. It's important to understand the difference and why you should choose the hard work of transformation over the easy path of change.

Change is a constant and an important force in our lives; we need to embrace change in order to go where God wants us to go next and in order to continue learning, growing, and discovering all our lives. However, change is not always the answer when you're asking the question, "What does God want of me?" The change we most often engage in is cosmetic. It's like rearranging the deck chairs on a large boat that's at sea; as soon as a big wave comes, they will easily slide and need to be rearranged again. Change is the constant activity that makes us feel like we're actually "doing something," when in reality, it is not as helpful as we'd like. Change is revising the surface features of your life without doing anything to what lies underneath. Making changes on the surface doesn't demand much of us. It doesn't ask us to confront beliefs that may not be valid any longer, or to take a hard look at grudges, fears, and prejudices that we may be harboring.

The root of the word "transformation" tells you all you need to know about it. The word comes from the Latin *transformare*, which, according to etymonline.com, means, "to make a thorough or dramatic change in the form, function, or character of." In other words, while change might alter how something looks or feels, transformation alters what something *is*. There's a huge difference.

As faith walkers, we're called on to undergo transformation. If you look at your life today and feel unhappy, lost, or dissatisfied—you might decide to change things. You might start working out, lose twenty-five pounds, and get a new wardrobe. Those are worthwhile changes to make, to be sure. But they will probably not change who you are—how you think, what you believe to be true about yourself and others, what you fear, or whether or not you are following your deepest passions. In order to become the person who is more aligned with the Creator's

Intent, you must not only change, but you must transform, and that means starting from within.

SICK AND TIRED OF BEING SICK AND TIRED

Transformation is not an external work. Instead, it begins internally, where consciousness and the Creator's Intent finally reach synchrony between who you've become and where you've ended up. There really is no instruction handbook or blueprint to show you how to transform your life, or a timeline warning when it will strike. Sometimes, the desire for transformation comes on suddenly, after you've reached a breaking point; other times, it can creep up on you for years as you toil in the same job, live in the same place, see the same people, and feel the same vague sense of, "I was meant for more than this." Some have said that transformation begins at the point where a person gets sick and tired of being sick and tired.

Albert Einstein has defined insanity as continuing to do the same thing but expecting different results. When it comes to changing the course of our lives, most of us are guilty as charged of continuing to do the same things but expecting different outcomes. We date the same kinds of people and then wonder why we always end up in the same kinds of relationships. We eat junk food to make ourselves feel better and then wonder why we can't lose weight. We procrastinate about going back to school and yet complain about being stuck in a dead-end job.

Getting a new haircut, going from glasses to contact lenses, and upgrading your wardrobe never produces new results in the long term because those measures don't change *who you are*. They don't take into account your need for purpose and significance. Too often we invest in these types of mild changes and then lay some heavy expectations on them. That's simply unrealistic. Your new haircut will not change your life! Losing twenty-five pounds is a terrific goal, but it won't change your underlying philosophy of life—only you can do that in your mind and spirit. Nor will new contact lenses give you the type of vision you need to navigate your life to a more meaningful and significant place. I'm not saying that outer changes are worthless; they're not. If getting in shape, dressing better, and whitening your teeth gives you more confidence, that's great. But don't fool yourself into believing that cosmetic changes will bring you the life you crave.

WHEREVER YOU GO, THERE YOU ARE

An important truth about transformation:

What brings you into alignment with the Creator's Intent may change depending on the life stage you are in.

We are not static beings, and while some lucky few may find a calling at an early age and remain fulfilled and centered in God's purpose for their entire lives, most of us won't. When I was younger, playing football brought me delight, meaning, and a sense of being "where I was supposed to be." But later, it lost that sense of purpose, so I moved on to a new stage of my life. In the future, who knows? I might move on to yet another stage. Where we are at twenty isn't always where God intends for us to be at forty-five. What feels right to you now may not feel right tomorrow, next week, or next year. That's okay.

Another reality of transformation is that change often disguises itself as transformation. I have a friend who thought she was undergoing a genuine transformation in her life because she moved fifteen hundred miles away from home. She was certain that relocating to a new part of the country would make her a different person. However, upon closer inspection of her life, she realized that even though her friends had changed, many of them still had the same attitudes and mind-sets as the ones back home. Upon stepping back and really looking, she realized that she had moved to a community very similar to the community she'd left, and even gotten the exact same type of job. She had changed her address and nothing else.

I call this the "wherever you go, there you are" syndrome. It means that no matter what superficial changes you undertake, until you change the fundamentals of who you are, you will still get the same results. Think of the many men and women who are desperate to get married because they believe that, somehow, the act of being married will change who they are. But it doesn't work that way, which is one of the reasons why so many marriages end in divorce. There's no magical threshold we can cross over to instantly become someone else.

However, we want to believe this to be true. We want to believe that we can reboot ourselves through one dramatic change. We want to believe that through half measures we will become the people God intends. But that's not the case, and we can make costly, chaotic, disruptive moves in our lives, with the false assumption that they will change us. Though my friend left a lot behind when she relocated, the disappointments and feelings of dissatisfaction in her life followed her. Though her zip code, neighborhood, and the faces of her friends all changed, there was no transformation.

While change is temporary, transformation has a greater sense of permanence. My friend who relocated fifteen hundred miles from home could easily have decided after one year that she'd had enough and moved back to where she'd started. Change is reversible because it's superficial. You're not risking much when you wear different clothes or date someone new, so it's very easy to abandon those changes when they don't deliver what you want. Low risk equals low return. Change is tempting because it's safe.

Transformation is frightening in part because it demands that we go "all in." You can't transform halfway, because transformation is more lasting. When you discover a new source of meaning in your life, alter what you believe about yourself and the world, or overcome a long-standing fear, there's no going back. It's not like you can hit some sort of cosmic reset button and be the person you once were. You're different down to your spirit. Your mind and heart are not the same. That's what scares many of us: the fear that if we let go of what we know and transform, we won't like what we find on the other end of that process.

Truth be told, you might not like everything you find. But I'm here to tell you that you will love *who you become.* Is it possible that if you turn your back on friends who have become toxic, or throw caution to the wind in order to risk everything and start your own business, that you'll find yourself lonely and broke for a while? Sure it is. Transformation is not easy. But it's also true that transformation is not about your circumstances changing; it's about *you* changing. And the person you become through the process of transformation will be braver, wiser, more passionate, more filled with purpose and energy, and closer to God than ever before. Transformation makes us the people we have always wanted to be.

Transformation 101

This chapter is not about negating the need for change, because we all make necessary and meaningful changes every day. There is a place in our lives for changes, and maybe your life only needs mild adjustments. However, whereas change merely modifies the existing process while producing the same or slightly modified results, transformation produces very different outcomes.

How do you know if the time is right for you to embark on a journey of transformation toward your Creator's Intent? Your instinct and emotions will guide you. If you're feeling unsatisfied, lost, and frustrated with your choices, transformation may be in order. If you're feeling like you can barely face another day of your current career, transformation could be at hand. If you have been hearing a voice for years telling you, "You were meant for more than this," but you never listened, maybe it's time to finally pay attention.

So what changes during a transformation?

- The things you believe to be true about yourself.
- The things you believe to be true about others.
- The things you believe to be true about how the world works.
- How you see relationships and people's choices.
- Your fears.
- Your perspective on the choices you've made in the past and why you made them.
- Your ability to see patterns in your own and others' behavior.
- Your ability to predict and change those patterns.
- How you embrace your passions.
- Your determination to follow your passion and purpose.
- Your ability to perceive God in your life.

Basically, transformation changes everything except your wardrobe, and you'll probably want to change that, too! We will talk more deeply about transformation as it relates to aligning yourself with the Creator's Intent as we move on, but below is a set of exercises and reflection questions that will help reveal some wisdom and personal insight about transformation as you begin to consider what you must do to transform.

BREAKING IT DOWN: GOING FOR TRANSFORMATION

Feel free to take out your journal and write down your thoughts, answers, and even concerns as you contemplate these points:

1. **Look at the core of who you are.** Confronting the blank page of transformation can leave you utterly confused. Where to start? Start by looking critically at the three aspects of yourself that define you. Answer these questions and figure out which answers are holding you back from the life you want:

   - What you think: What are your habits of thought? Are they empowering or defeating?
   - What you feel: How do you handle your emotions? Do you let them overwhelm you or do you keep them in perspective?
   - What you believe: What are your deep beliefs about yourself and your worth? What do you believe is your best, highest purpose?

2. **Your life creates ripples that affect others.** Your life is a stone in the pond of God's creation, and you impact others whether you know it or not. Transformation is about becoming a better version of you, but at the same time, don't ignore your impact on others. You're not responsible for how your friends and family feel about you moving on to something greater (and many people may not be happy, because your success will highlight their failures), but it is wise to consider how your transformation will affect people who you care about. You could start by making a list of these people and then reflect on how your transformation may affect each of them.

3. **You are who you hang out with.** Transformation means being critical and discerning about the relationships in your life. Grow and nurture any existing relationships that inspire and build you up. End those that are draining you dry, leading you down an unrighteous path, or making you

feel bad about yourself. Get to know and befriend people who lift you up, want to see you be greater, and who bring you health, healing, and love. To look honestly at your relationships will require courage and you may want to begin by reviewing the list you made in point two above and clearly discerning which of these important people truly inspire confidence and encourage your aspirations.

4. **Accept that you will be afraid and uncomfortable.** Transformation is about risking it all, and that will take you far from your comfort zone. You will feel like you're in free-fall sometimes. You'll be tempted to turn back and reverse course. Be strong. Fear and apprehension are God's signals that we are on the right path to rebirth. They are signals that you are escaping the gravity of sameness, lethargy, and predictability. Embrace those feelings and persist on your path.

5. **Understand that you could not have chosen any other way.** When we confront ourselves and see the effects of the choices we've made in the past, it's very common to beat ourselves up for those choices. From the perspective of a transformed mind, we get furious at ourselves for not taking action sooner. This kind of self-recrimination is not only unhealthy but unnecessary. The person you are becoming may see the folly of your choices, but in the past, they were the vehicle for the lessons that have led you where you are. Accept your past choices and find the lessons in each of them, and then forgive yourself. Writing out a story in your journal about a past action or choice that holds you back can close the old wound; the process of writing can offer healing and learning by allowing you to see your past more objectively and to tap into your self-compassion. At the end of your story, write: "I'm complete and ready to forgive myself. I'm ready to move on."

At a Glance: Transformation Versus Change

1. Change and transformation are both useful and necessary. Change is less personally invasive, and the results are easily adjustable or even reversible. A life transformation, on the other hand, is extremely invasive—spiritually, emotionally, and physically—and the results have a more permanent effect on your destiny and direction.

2. Transformation is an internal job, not an external one. Transforming your life begins in the mind and heart.

3. Transformation comes at a cost. This cost is the abandonment or total loss of many things and people, including your former self.

4. Transformations demand that you go all in. Your comfort zone will be disturbed. Transformation is about risking it all to discover the new you, the one your Creator intended.

CHAPTER 2: FIND CONGRUENCE

"We are born believing. A man bears beliefs as a tree bears apples."

—Ralph Waldo Emerson

Along with my career as a professional football player, it's worth noting that each of my siblings is a good athlete as well: three were college football players (two played in the NFL), one was a college wrestler, and one was a long-distance track runner. What is amazing, however, is that most of our extended family was nonathletic but had amazing natural vocal and musical talents equal to our athletic talents. As they supported us at our athletic events, we enjoyed supporting their musical endeavors. While I couldn't carry a tune if you gave me a knapsack to hold it in, I admired their ability to vocally harmonize with one another and create rhythms to make beautiful music.

A musical harmony is when at least two different notes come together on the same pitch, and rhythm is the pattern and cadence of each musical piece. The combinations of harmonies that keep up with the rhythms are the key to making good music, and in many respects, understanding the Creator's Intent of your life is a similar process. The harmony of your parts (gifts, beliefs, efforts, etc.) must keep up with God's cadence/rhythm if something good is going to happen. This is finding *congruence*:

The place where your life is in harmony with God's rhythm.

Finding this compatibility aligns your gifts with God's purpose and produces significance, meaning, and fulfillment in your life. While it's possible to achieve congruence with the Creator, there are many variables that get in the way, and none attack congruence more ferociously than faulty belief systems. Here is an example.

Nearly eighteen years ago I was a part of an inspiring group of leaders and mentors who were passionate about the city of San Diego and its youth. After weeks of strategizing, we decided that it would be beneficial to expand the creative horizons of a group of San Diego–area inner-city teenagers. We thought an effective way to do this would be to set up monthly field trips to museums, local colleges, art galleries, county events, and things of that sort—experiences that they could not have had in their own communities.

To keep our costs down, we opted to take the kids to lunch at familiar yet inexpensive eating places like McDonald's and TGI Fridays, and asked the parents to give their children five to eight dollars to cover the cost of meals. We hoped we would expose these kids to different experiences in life without taxing their parents financially. Our team was excited about the trips, only to be outdone by the excitement of the teenagers when we told them of our intentions. However, to take the children off the church campus, we needed parental consent, so we set up a sign-up station. But approximately three weeks before the first trip we were shocked to find that fewer than five children had signed up!

We were nervous: we had booked and paid for guides and tours and arranged transportation and special treats, but it seemed that no one was participating. About one week before the first trip (with no more sign-ups) we called an emergency meeting to determine what had gone wrong. Did we market it ineffectively? Was there a community conflict with one of the venues? Was there strife among the teens or, worse, among the parents? After eliminating most of those possibilities we called another emergency meeting, but this time we invited the parents, hoping to find out how we could address any concerns they may have had. We thought that perhaps they didn't know that admission to the places we wanted to take their children was free, or perhaps something about our communication concerned them. But when we met with the parents and learned the truth, we were saddened.

The primary reason for the low sign-up rate was because many of the parents assumed they could not afford the trip because of the part of the city we were taking their children to. Some of the museums were in affluent areas of the San Diego region, and the parents believed that the McDonald's in La Jolla would be more expensive than the McDonald's in the part of the city they lived in. Furthermore, they believed that their children wouldn't fit in in those environments or know how to behave, understand, or enjoy the attractions because they were too different—too "urban." It was a heartbreaking example of disempowering beliefs in action.

Fortunately for those young people, we were able to clear up some of the misconceptions that were floating around. We assured the parents that the food at the McDonald's in La Jolla was no more expensive than the same meal in their communities, and we assured them that not only would their children do well in an environment different from their norm but the experience would challenge the communities they visited as much as it would challenge their children. The trips went forward and were very successful.

How many of us are shaped by environments similar to that one? How many of us have beliefs that limit our thoughts, potential, experiences, and ultimately our life outcomes? Imagine how many good employees have been passed over for promotions because their superiors subscribed to limited belief systems concerning color, race, or gender? How many talented individuals will never reach their great potential to be doctors or lawyers or artists because they were taught that a high school diploma was the highest they could or should aim for or that their talents weren't good enough?

What limits have you been trained to believe in? All men are no good? A thirty-thousand-dollar-a-year job is all you're worth? Disagreements in a relationship are resolved by violence? Stepparenting is not "real" parenting? What limits have been trained into you that keep you from experiencing maximum freedom? Furthermore, is your current environment reinforcing those beliefs so that you never question them? Beliefs become destiny, so it's time to start asking yourself what you believe and why you believe it, and then what you can do to change beliefs that are stealing your power and robbing you of the destiny that God has in mind for you.

CONGRUENCE WITH THE CREATOR

Are you happy in your life? Do you have the vitality, peace, and spiritual well-being that you desire? Do you feel fulfilled? If not, then it's likely that you are not operating in congruence with God's intent for you. God has His Creator's Intent; you have your own plans and ideas for your life. But when the two clash, there is disharmony and dysfunction. Only when your intent and the Creator's Intent are congruent and moving in the same direction can you function optimally. Only then will you find meaning and purpose in what you do. Only then will you find true happiness and joy. Only then will the fruits of your labors yield prosperity, physical comfort, and aid to others. To be the person God intends you to be, you must bring your own intent into alignment with the Creator's Intent.

You may feel that no one understands how scary and hard resetting faulty beliefs can be. I do. You may feel like you will be stretched far outside your comfort zone, risking potential failure. You will. So make no mistake about it: reconfiguring your life to find congruence with the Creator is an adjustment and an act of faith. If you're not sure, remember this:

God believes in you even if you don't believe in Him.

God sees you as having virtually no limits; there are no obstacles that can keep you from achieving congruence with Him. Don't let the limits or obstacles of your past beliefs keep you from actualizing your potential.

Can you imagine having more resources around you than you could ever use up? That is already happening inside you. You just need to see it and release it. In Maya Angelou's book *I Know Why the Caged Bird Sings*, she uses the metaphor of a caged bird—created to fly but confined to a cage—as a means to express her feelings and emotions while she overcame the trauma of prejudices and racism, identity issues, and rape, in a male-dominated and newly desegregated South.

She ultimately emerges as a woman of great dignity and a proud mother, and Angelou's autobiographical story represents the struggles of many people, particularly black women who were just like a bird in a cage: equipped and capable to do so much more than the cage would allow. The bird doesn't sing out of boredom as if it has nothing to do or contribute, but rather it wants to be free to soar! Paul Laurence Dunbar's poem "Sympathy" inspired Angelou's book title:

I know why the caged bird sings, ah me . . .
It is not a carol of joy or glee

What "cages" do you need to be free from so you can fly? When there is no freedom to be physically and emotionally congruent with the Creator's Intent for your life, it can lead to a feeling of being trapped. You may be caged by your belief systems, and bad belief systems will prevent you from ever finding true congruence with God. Is that you? If so, it's time to transform your thinking and get you out of those cages in your mind, one belief system at a time, and emerge as an active participant in your destiny.

When you are able to reprogram your mind and reset your beliefs fully, you will experience the blessing of being more in alignment, and possibly total congruence. That is the blessed state where you believe in yourself with the same surety and faith that God believes in you, and you are in step with Him. God doesn't doubt you; He knows exactly what He created in you and what your full potential really is. When you reach congruence, you will find doors opening in your life as never before. You will find relationships that are rich, deep, and rewarding. In the face of life's adversities, you will find opportunities coming your way, and you will experience confidence and self-love that you have never known. That is God's gift.

How do we align ourselves with the Creator's Intent? We need to take an honest look at our limiting beliefs and reprogram or reset our minds to match with our higher spiritual source. When we are not attuned to ourselves, we are ultimately not attuned to the Creator's Intent. A major barrier to this attunement is our beliefs, the beliefs that limit and close us off from what we are truly meant to become. Perhaps the most important thing you can know about beliefs is that your belief system is your personal thermostat.

BELIEFS ARE YOUR THERMOSTAT

As you know, a thermostat controls the temperature of a room based on input from the environment. A thermostat keeps the environment at a constant temperature; when something makes the room hotter or cooler, it's the thermostat's job to adjust the incoming air in order to bring the temperature back to that preset level.

The late Brian Klemmer, international consultant, speaker, and friend, used to teach that our "belief systems are like a thermostat." And boy, was he correct! Our belief systems work the same way. The beliefs you hold about yourself and the world—your limits, what you can and can't do, and so on—set your base temperature. Then, no matter what you do, those beliefs will drive your actions and won't stop until they bring you back to the level that you believe is where you belong. For example, if you believe that your hard work is worth a salary of forty thousand dollars and not a cent more, your belief system will not let you get past that income level. Because of your beliefs, you'll achieve only what you believe you should have. You'll pass on opportunities. You'll quit good jobs. Your beliefs won't let you rest spiritually or emotionally until you have satisfied what you believe about yourself—in some cases until you have returned to the temperature at which your beliefs tell you that you belong! This may lead you to underachieve.

One perfect example of this mentality is the story of how the Children of Israel refused to enter their sought-after Promised Land. After four hundred years of being slaves in Egypt, the Israelites miraculously escaped Egypt under Moses's guidance and set off to a new life. Free to build a life for themselves, one with endless possibilities, they were led to a land called Canaan, where it was promised they would prosper. Numbers 13 in the Bible tells of the time when Moses and his brother, Aaron, brought the Hebrews to Canaan, and how they refused to enter for fear that it was a wilderness where they would be slain by armies they could not defeat. Instead of accepting the challenge and the promise of their success, they rejected the Lord's guarantee and faith in a new future. In fact, the Hebrews very nearly chose a new leader to take them back into bondage in Egypt. The Israelites could not shed their old belief that they were incapable of freedom and prospering in Canaan, and they suffered for it.

Your belief systems control your level of faith. Most people will only produce what they believe of themselves and not much more—they will only drive themselves to the limit of their set expectations. Going back to the thermostat metaphor, your faith has its own temperature gauge: the place you believe you should operate and extend your faith to achieve. But this also works in reverse. So let's say that you surpass your "faith temperature" and your perceived abilities; your belief system's thermostat will then cause you to "cool" yourself off, bringing you back to that base level—the place where you believe you belong. I see it too regularly, the self-sabotaging behaviors of very capable people who simply don't believe they should go any further, diminishing their talents and confidence.

Beliefs are the steady state at which we always settle, and there's no fighting them. When you're high up but you believe you don't deserve to be, you'll trip yourself up in order to get down to where you believe you should be. No matter what you do, a person who believes that they will always be in relationships with losers will always find a way to end good relationships with good people to find a loser. Only until they change their beliefs and reset their thermostat—and find congruence with the Creator—will they truly make a permanent alteration to their habitual patterns.

A pastor friend of mine leads a wonderful church in California. The church he started was birthed out of the limits of his father, who was also a pastor but who never had more than a hundred fifty members of his church, was always financially strapped, and struggled with his congregation month in, month out, over one issue or another—usually about a poor decision he had made. Well, my friend's church joined an organization that helped with systems for growth and held his church financially accountable, so he wouldn't expand too slowly or too quickly without sufficient resources. It didn't take long for his church to grow and soon surpass that of his father. It grew to more than three hundred members.

His church attracted a wealth of qualified leaders who could see his vision and help him bring it to fruition with a minimal amount of congregational drama. Because of these and other wise decisions, he watched his church grow numerically, financially, and spiritually . . . and then he hit his belief system limit. What ensued was tragic. He worried that he didn't have enough control of things based on what he was conditioned to think.

Over a minor disagreement, he ended up leaving the organization of leaders who had helped build his church, which caused many of his most stable members to distance themselves from the church. A series of poor decisions led to the regrettable demise of his otherwise healthy ministry. Today, despite being a gifted speaker and visionary, he continues to struggle to build something greater. His ministry has returned to the default setting determined by his limiting beliefs. His belief thermostat has restored the constant temperature, even though he could be capable of so much more.

WHAT DO YOU BELIEVE?

One of my father's most often used phrases was, "Just making it." I cannot tell you how many times I remember hearing that growing up. If you ever asked him how he was doing, his response was, "Just making it." If you asked him how the family was, "We are just making it." It wasn't a positive or negative phrase; it was just a seemingly harmless but habitual phrase he used.

For whatever reason, because we were a lower-middle-class family and money issues were constantly the topic of conversations in our home, I always applied that phrase to his financial situation, which, as a child, was "our" financial situation. In my head, we were always just making it. While there may have been some truth to that during my childhood, I never realized how this phrase would frame my long-term belief systems. Subconsciously, I accepted the "just making it" mentality, which led me to believe that it was normal to be just making it financially.

As a struggling college student it fit my belief system just fine. But when I got to the NFL, my financial world changed. I was in a position where I no longer needed to "just make it." In fact, I was financially thriving and had abundance all around me. Sadly, though, my belief thermostat was stuck on just making it. My first few years in the NFL, I spent and spent, and spent some more. I got to the off-season and realized that I put myself in a tight financial situation. And I mean really tight! It took me a few days of being disappointed in myself to realize that it wasn't all the usual excuses—poor money management, lack of financial education, poor discipline, etc. While to some degree it was those things, it was also that I operated under a poor belief system. I created a "just making it" situation for myself, because I always believed that was where I belonged.

What you believe will determine your limits. More to the point:

What you have been conditioned to believe will determine what you permit yourself to achieve.

What do you believe about yourself, and where did those beliefs come from? In what areas of your life are you limiting yourself? Each of us has areas where we sorely underachieve, not because of ability but because of belief. We harbor unconscious but powerful beliefs that we can only go so far and no farther. We're unworthy of love, too weak for success, we're screwups who inevitably mess up the best opportunities—the self-defeating, self-limiting beliefs we adopt are endless. But beliefs like these are not the products of God's thinking—He does not put anything into your mind or spirit that is not intended to elevate you.

Self-limiting beliefs come from man, from ourselves. And if we've imposed those beliefs on ourselves, we can also change them. Philippians 4:8–9 says, "Finally, brethren, whatever things are true, whatever things are noble, whatever things are just, whatever things are pure, whatever things are lovely, whatever things are of good report, if there is any virtue and if there is anything praiseworthy—meditate on these things. The things which you learned and received and heard and saw in me, these do, and the God of peace will be with you." We can turn our minds to negative beliefs—or away from them. It's our choice.

Think about it. Where and from whom did your underlying beliefs come from? Did they begin with repeated messages you heard from your parents or teachers? Did you have an early relationship that taught you not to trust? Beliefs come from patterns that are ingrained in our minds after much repetition. Our experiences reinforce them. For example, if you were told when you were a child that you were not smart enough to succeed in college, a belief took root in your mind. Then if you went to college anyway but struggled in your first class, that belief may have been reinforced. Now it's anchored deep in your subconscious. It's been validated. You don't even have to think about it, you just know: *I'm not smart enough*. Resetting your thermostat is about questioning those habitual beliefs.

Have you considered what you say to yourself that reinforces your self-imposed limits? Now that you understand that you have some beliefs that aren't serving you well, what do you intend to do about them? An important first step is to challenge any faulty beliefs. Before you can consistently produce new, different results, you must rewrite your operating system, so to speak. You must let go of disempowering, false beliefs and adopt new beliefs that reflect the greatness that God has placed within you. When you recognize that your thermometer is set and you've reached your max, you must reset your thermometer to accept higher temperatures, lifting the bar of your expectations.

Our self-defeating beliefs are born of lies, fear, anxiety, and an unrealistic expectation of what the world has in store for us. For proof, ask yourself this: How many times have you feared something in the future, yet when that thing came your fears proved to be groundless? Whether it was a work assignment, an interview, a test, a doctor's appointment, or a date, we fear that we are much less powerful and capable than we really are.

In her book *A Return to Love*, Marianne Williamson writes, "Our deepest fear is not that we are inadequate. Our deepest fear is that we are powerful beyond measure. It is our light, not our darkness, that most frightens us. We ask ourselves, Who am I to be brilliant, gorgeous, talented, and fabulous? Actually, who are you *not* to be? You are a child of God. Your playing small does not serve the world."

REDEFINING SUCCESS

One specific area that can strongly affect our belief thermostat is how we define the word "success." Ask yourself: What has shaped how I define success—television shows, teachers, a favorite celebrity, a social group, a church, or a guru? What images and influencers have affected how you define success? This is important for your development. If the people that shaped your definition of success don't know any substantive things about you, such as your personality, talents, background, etc., it is likely that they can't offer a substantive definition of success for you.

Success should be based upon maximizing the intended use of your gifts and what they produce. When a person has been able to find self-meaning, she has found more than success, she has found significance. So erase what you've seen on TV, read in magazines, and seen on the Internet. Cars, boats, and party life don't equate to success. Successful relationships, responsible parenting, community action, ideas and solutions, etc., operate in a higher consciousness of existential contribution, where the reward is not money or applause but the action or product itself. Do you still value your success based on how much money you make? How many "attaboys" you get? If so, you may need to redefine success.

Where I grew up in the Midwest, mills and factories offered the most-sought-after jobs. Anheuser-Busch and the General Motors plant were the two biggest employers in my city, and it was not uncommon to hear adults encourage high school seniors to "go down to the factory and get a good job." Other advice included, "graduate from high school, go to college, and get a real good job like a doctor or lawyer, or learn a trade." Not to discount the thousands of hard workers who keep those factories running or the good work of honest doctors, lawyers, and tradespeople, but what a limited view of success! Kids from my hometown weren't encouraged to find their purpose and chase their vision; they were encouraged to go out and start earning money to create stability. To many in our area, the only option for success was a factory job with benefits and a pension.

Unfortunately, many of them raced off to get those jobs and became stable but miserable. Then when the markets turned, they were laid off and became doubly miserable! Consequently, when the factories closed down, they took more than our stability; they also took the joys, hopes, and purpose from entire communities. If you find the Creator's Intent in factory work, that's wonderful; many honest and good people do. But I think you can agree that telling young souls that working in an industry is practically their "only choice" amounts to throwing a monkey wrench into their possibilities and ultimately into God's plans.

Too many of us relinquish the hopes and purpose of our lives into the hands of well-meaning parents, mentors, teachers, and bosses. But when you let your life's meaning be defined by someone else instead of by your Creator's Intent, you set yourself up for disappointment, frustration, and heartache. Start asking:

- Does my picture of personal success make me feel meaningful or just successful?
- Do I need to adjust my perception of my personal success to match my sense of meaningfulness?
- If so, what do those adjustments look like?

These answers will begin to guide you in the direction of the Creator's Intent and on your road to finding personal success that is unique to you.

Resetting Your Thermostat

You can discover that brilliant, fabulous self by challenging and resetting those faulty beliefs that hold you back and replacing them with beliefs that maximize, rather than minimize, you.

How do you challenge faulty beliefs? Well, your beliefs are unconscious settings for how you view yourself and the world, so the first thing you must do is make them *conscious*. Drag them into the light. Confront them. Start by making these lists and answering these questions honestly, openly, and courageously in your journal:

1. Make a list of categories or subcategories that are important in your life (money, relationships, your ability to be a good spouse/friend/parent, family, religion/God, society/world, people of different ethnicities, areas of failure, artistic interests, etc.).
2. Write out a statement of what your current and truest beliefs are about each category you listed.

3. For each belief ask yourself: Where did it originate? Why do I still hold on to it and operate in it?

4. How has this belief contributed to where I am in my life today?

5. Is this belief helping me or hurting me as I move toward my personal or professional goals?

As you do this exercise you will begin to realize how your thoughts and beliefs are affecting your life, whether positively or negatively. It will help you begin to separate the beliefs that work from those that work against you. You want to pay attention to and develop empowering beliefs that help you find synergy and congruence with the Creator's Intent for your life. You need to confront disempowering beliefs that take you further from your purpose; those disempowering beliefs are always false. That's because God has planted seeds of greatness in you that make you strong, viable, and necessary. Those seeds are different for everyone; some people are destined to grow into political leaders or world-famous artists, while others are purposed with becoming great as teachers, gardeners, or parents. The scope or cultural image of what you are meant to be great at doesn't matter; it's the fact that you have the potential for wonders within you that matters. But we get so caught up in fear, competition, and beating ourselves up for our failures that sometimes we never stop to question the beliefs that hold us back.

Resetting your personal belief thermostat and aligning your congruence with the Creator's Intent means practicing and doing the following:

1. **State each negative belief out loud:** Speaking it makes it real. You need to hear for yourself what you believe. For example, you might say, "I believe that I don't have the drive and ability to start my own business."

2. **Call out how that belief has harmed you:** You might say, "That belief has kept me from ever pursuing all the good business ideas I've had, even the opportunities that came my way."

3. **State the untruth of the belief:** "This belief is not true."

4. **Invert the belief:** For example, say, "I believe that I do have the drive, passion, and skill to successfully start my own business."

5. **State a courageous next step you will perform to demonstrate this new, positive belief:** For example, say, "I will demonstrate this true belief by telling my best friend of my fear and intentions for accountability, then I will share my business idea with a potential partner."

6. **Repeat:** Remember, you're reprogramming your mind, and that takes time. Repetition and remembrance is important. One of my favorite Bible verses is Romans 10:17, ". . . faith comes by hearing . . ." You need to repeat these steps from time to time to remind yourself that you are in a battle to change your beliefs. The greatest tactic an enemy can employ is the one that causes you to forget that he is your enemy. So put these beliefs in clear sight, rehearse your new expectations, and remember: repetition established the negative beliefs in the first place, and repetition will help replace them. Build your faith to work for you and not against you!

7. **Act:** Finally, this exercise is meaningless unless you follow through on your promise to demonstrate this new belief. Essentially, you must prove to yourself that you can live up to your stated empowering belief. So take action and don't give up.

BREAKING IT DOWN: CONGRUENCE WITH GOD

God believes in you. He created you as a powerful expression of His greatness, full of His Divine essence, and then He strategically placed you in a terrestrial world that is beckoning for you to assert yourself with authority and power. If you do, your greatest potential can be achieved. The environment is ready for you to contribute your best, and this is the Creator's doing. It's clear that Gods believes in you; however, the most important questions to ask yourself are:

- Do you believe in yourself?
- Do you believe in what has been created in you?

When you are in congruence with the will of God, your atmosphere, though it may protest, will concede victories to you. The greater our ability to believe that we are a part of God's creative ideal, with no limits, the greater our opportunities to achieve our fullest potential and discover joy and fulfillment. Like a child with no filter, you must learn to recapture the purity of belief. Children aspire to do outrageous things: fly, go to the moon, discover magical powers, or jet on a "super plane" from Missouri to California in fifteen minutes (at least that's what my niece dreams of!).

Children's beliefs may be untethered to reality, but their dreams are based on the belief that there are no limits to what they can do. Read what God thinks about you and your potential: "Now to him who is able to do exceedingly abundantly above all that we ask or think, according to the power that works in us" (Ephesians 3:20). This is a great verse for validating how you should disregard limitations upon yourself, your potential, and your dreams. When you submit to God and work in hand with Him and His design for you, you will have access to an immeasurable ability to produce something beyond your wildest imagination, something God-worthy.

- Now, imagine what you could do if you took those same limitless beliefs and applied them to the skill, knowledge, and work ethic that you possess?
- Take the above verse, Ephesians 3:20, and make it your affirmation. Practice it in one area in your life this week, and notice (or write) what feelings and experiences emerge.

AT A GLANCE: FINDING CONGRUENCE

1. Our beliefs shape our limits. There are not many things that affect your ascension as profoundly as what you believe.
2. Congruence means finding your rhythm with God and His will for your life. A major key to discovering the Creator's Intent for your life is keeping up with the Divine pace of your life.
3. Beliefs control the thermostat of your life. How hard you pursue your passions will be determined by how much your core beliefs drive you to have them.
4. You cannot outrun your beliefs. Belief systems must be recognized, confronted, and then accepted or altered. You can move far away, but your beliefs come with you. Find out why you do what you do and prepare a plan to empower your new belief system.

5. Limiting beliefs can be reprogrammed. You are not doomed to a life of limitations. Beliefs can be adjusted to better serve the destiny of your life.

6. Success in the eyes of the world is a fleeting goal; you should redefine your goals around achieving personal significance and meaning.

Chapter 3: Lead With Your Pivot

"If we could change ourselves, the tendencies in the world would also change. As a man changes his own nature, so does the attitude of the world change towards him. This is the divine mystery supreme."

—Gandhi

A while ago, a group of friends and I were hanging out at the shopping mall. In the midst of me shopping for shoes and my friends shopping for what seemed like everything else in the mall, we somehow became separated. The last place I remembered being with them was at Neiman Marcus. When I started to drift to other retail stores during my shoe search, I lost track of where I was in relation to Neiman Marcus. Needing to get my bearings, I went to the map kiosk, and I found a big red X and the words "You Are Here" in bold lettering. Great.

Unfortunately, I was nearly at the opposite end of the mall from where I had started. And how many items I had accumulated was even more telling of my state of being lost. Though I started my quest looking for only a new pair of shoes, I ended up with sunglasses, a shirt, and a few other items I neither needed nor had intended to buy. While I was standing by the kiosk, all I could do was wonder, *How in the world did I end up* here, *so far away from* there? And furthermore, *What is my first step to get back?* When I figured it out, I had to pivot and do a one-eighty, heading back in the direction of my friends.

It's a funny story, but it illustrates an important point about you and the Creator's Intent: Why are you where you are in your life? When you survey the inventory of your life and ask, "How did I end up here, so far from where I intended to be?" you realize life is a long journey, and on a long journey even tiny errors in your course can lead you to someplace you didn't intend.

How does one end up a janitor when he set out to become a doctor? How does another wind up as a single parent when she aspired to have a loving marriage? How did he end up overweight when he set out to live a healthy life? Have you ever wondered about the events and decisions of your life that may have steered you off the road of destiny you always saw yourself traveling? If so, you're not alone. Just like me at the mall, unintentionally and without effort, we can end up wayward and off course, loaded down with things we didn't intend to pick up along the way. At the mall it was sunglasses and items of clothing, but in life it can be a list of serious issues, such as health problems, bad relationships, regrets, debts, hurts, disappointments, and so on. Together, this baggage tells us that, despite our best intentions, we have not become the people we set out to be.

I've noticed that there are two types of people in life, and perhaps, you may have noticed it, too. There are people who become lost in the changing circumstances of their lives and never find their way back to what they intended to be. These are the ones that give up, surrender, and even chalk it up to "God's will." Then there are people who seem to roll with the punches. When life sends them a surprise, they go with it and rise above it. They follow a bad decision with a good decision. They don't get sidetracked by the same distractions, and they even manage to focus their way through new emerging ones.

What separates those people from the rest of us? Three qualities:

1. They take responsibility for where they are. They don't blame anyone or anything else. They hold themselves responsible and accountable.
2. They have a belief system that tells them they deserve success and that they can rise above any situation.
3. They're focused and intentional on having their desired results. They avoid distractions and make wise decisions.

We've already talked about the power of beliefs, your mental and spiritual thermostat. I trust that by now you know your beliefs have the power to elevate you or bring you down. It is important to take responsibility for where you are and who you've become, so that you can become more.

THE PIVOT

Have you given in to fears? The fear of failure? The fear of success? The fear of what others will think or say? The fear of freedom and responsibility?

Have you decided whom you are willing to include? Whom you are unwilling to rid yourself of?

Have you considered and reconciled yourself to the decisions you've made over the years? Have you forgiven and let go of past actions?

These are important questions to consider if you are to accept responsibility for where you are and move forward. Some of it may be difficult to hear and admit to yourself, but it's all necessary. However, what then? What happens after you take responsibility for your past choices? Surely, looking in the mirror and admitting to yourself and God, "Yes, I did that," isn't the end, is it? No. It's just the beginning.

The summer of 1993 was a particularly difficult summer for me. I was a sophomore in college, an emerging football star, with lots of extra time and freedom—a bad combination! This particular day a group of teammates and I went to a nightclub to party and, for me and my friends, not much good happened hanging out late in those types of places. That night was not a good one for me. I got into a heated argument on the dance floor, a fistfight ensued, and the kid ended up hurt pretty badly. That was a night of maximum anxiety and uncertainty as the police carried me away in cuffs in the police wagon. After having endured a series of serious tongue-lashings from my parents and coaches, I sat in my apartment overlooking downtown Madison, Wisconsin, taking inventory of my life. How did I end up here, with a nightclubbing lifestyle? What kind of environment had I created for myself that made it so easy for me to resolve conflicts by fighting? How come none of my friends had stopped me? Were we enablers?

I did not have all the answers, but I determined that I was ultimately responsible for my situation, for the kid's condition, and, most important, for whatever personal adjustments I needed to make moving forward. Identifying what gets you off course isn't enough; identifying the problem *and then* planning a new course are necessary for real transformation. For all of us, trying to find our way to the Creator's Intent and live the life that God has in mind for us, one truth should guide us:

The right change in how we think or act today can change all the outcomes of tomorrow.

I call this the *pivot*. It's the point on which everything turns in a different direction. The pivot is a thought pattern, a choice, or an action that you decide you will handle differently from this point forward, something from which many of your life's outcomes flow downstream. It's the thing or series of things that can change everything.

Your pivot could be as simple as saying yes to things that you have always said no to, or calling the personal trainer you've been meaning to call for the last five years so you can start to get in shape. It could be confronting a parent over something in your past that haunts you, or setting up an automatic withdrawal from your paycheck that goes into savings for retirement. It could be deciding to confront one thing you're afraid of each month. Your pivot place could happen anywhere at anytime, but it is when the ship starts to sail in a different direction.

The pivot is an initial choice or decision that can lead to many benefits in your future, whether financial, physical, emotional, or professional. So what could your pivot be? What one thing could you begin doing differently today that will snowball into improved results and happiness for you tomorrow? More to the point, what could you do that will start taking you closer to the Creator's Intent? Keep in mind that a pivot can be:

- A thought
- A habit
- A conversation
- The start of a new type of relationship
- The end of something (and the beginning of something new)
- Relocating
- A decision to move on, or forgive, or stand your ground

However, you must do three things to ensure that your pivot is more than just a temporary feel-good measure that does nothing for you in the long term:

1. **You must stick to it.** If you decide that your pivot is confronting an unhealthy relationship, then you must decide for yourself whether to turn the relationship

around through honest work and attention, or to let it go altogether. This could be frightening, but there's no other way to move in a different direction. If you decide that your pivot is giving up alcohol, then you must make yourself accountable for staying sober. You can't stop drinking for a month and then say, "Maybe just one." Is this hard? Yes. Changing things in your life is hard. But you only have to start with one change, the right change, to see innumerable benefits. Think of it as making a wise investment in your destiny.

2. **You must tie your pivot to what you want to transform.** Pivot on something that matters. To pivot is to choose to honor your own interests for the sake of moving closer to your destiny. It is not a series of selfish decisions but ones that help you to become the best version of yourself in order to serve humanity more efficiently. For example, if you've been overweight for most of your life and being more trim and fit would allow you to enjoy and participate more in recreation time with your children, then your pivot might be saying, "I will hire a personal trainer and start eating a healthy diet as of right now to transform my body, so I will be able to spend quality recreation time with my children." It won't do you as much good to pivot on something that's trivial or even vain.

3. **Your pivot must lead you toward the Creator's Intent.** Anytime you pivot, you turn *away* from something and *toward* something else. What you pivot toward is critical because it will be the object of your next pursuit. Using the example of my mall excursion, it would not have served me to move from one location to another store, if I continued to be lost. Ideally, you want to pivot in

a direction where you sense the most congruency with God and His intentions for your life. Even if you must pause for a season to discern and understand the lessons of your misstep, which direction you move toward after you pivot is an important decision.

RESPONSIBILITY LEADS YOUR PIVOT

Remember that a pivot is a point when we change a habit, make a decision, or take a different action that starts us in a new direction in our lives. And a key dimension to moving to that pivot point, and then sticking with it, is how we take responsibility for our past, present, and future decisions. You must accept responsibility for where you are or where you are not. You cannot change something until you have ownership of it; it's like trying to return something to a store without a receipt. No ownership, no do-over! Accept responsibility for the choices, actions, thoughts, and reactions that have gotten you to any of the unsatisfactory places in your life. Look in the mirror and say, "Yes, I did that."

Often, I find that people of faith are not especially good at this. We tend to be too fatalistic in our view of the world, assuming that whatever happens is God's will. "Oh well," we'll say, "that must have happened because God doesn't want me to become this or that." The Creator's Intent is the manifestation of God's will, but how you express your life is not up to God. It's up to you! You must participate in your life for the Creator's Intent to be fully expressed.

If we're not using God as a ready excuse, we're pointing the finger at someone else—our parents, spouse, teacher, employer, or society. That's just dodging responsibility. Don't blame God or others for your regrets, poor choices, or the times you decided to give up too soon. Your life is exactly that: *your* life. You cannot blame others for its progression. You own your choices. Only by admitting ownership of your mistakes can you correct them. God and life itself give you grace to make mistakes, so don't ignore your mistakes, and dishonor the grace offered to you. We all miss the mark sometimes—take ownership of that.

Let's start by being specific about why you are responsible for the place you're at today. Make a list of the things you did and the decisions that you made that affected where you are right now in your life, the reasons why you did not pursue your Creator's Intent. Some examples:

- I often don't tell people what I really think and feel.
- I would have benefited from waiting before I made this major decision.
- I didn't budget my finances well and often wasted my resources on needless things.
- I honestly haven't tried to go after what is in my heart.
- I had a tragic thing happen to me and I can't manage to get past it.
- I don't believe I can get what I want.
- I have intentionally ignored or disagreed with the truest yearnings of my heart.
- I don't know what to do or how to find a purpose.

The point of this exercise isn't to make you feel terrible, though you might. Confronting our own culpability in our failures—our unhappiness and sense of being lost—is painful. That's why we avoid doing it and find something—anything—else to blame! The truth is that you will never defeat a problem you are unwilling to confront. So the purpose of making this list and honestly, openly confronting the decisions you've made and their consequences is to awaken in you two incredibly powerful realities:

1. If you have the capacity to make poor choices, you also have the ability to make wise ones.
2. You can change your future immediately by deciding right now to change how you make decisions.

I remember when the housing crisis of the early 2000s hit. Housing investors like myself were scrambling to sell all the overvalued properties they had. The financial numbers got so confusing and chaotic that I had to call my CPA for help. In the quest to help me figure out what I needed to do to fix my situation, he asked me to bring him everything related to my investment portfolio—receipts, deeds, credit card statements, bank papers, you name it. It was so much stuff that I needed to search on old computers, in drawers, and in dusty boxes. I had to do some real digging to get the information he needed.

Doing so opened some old wounds, revealing some serious mistakes I had made. But it was necessary because my CPA needed all of that information so he could determine what my current status was. Only then could he help me get where I needed to be. It was time consuming, laborious, and even embarrassing, but guess what? He got me steady and helped move me to a healthier place in my real-estate business.

This will be the challenge for many of you as well—digging deep into your past, unveiling some of your less favorable choices and decisions, and being transparent. You will discover your dream only after you face what mistakes you've made in the past.

We get caught up in currents in our lives, one leading to the next, and it sometimes becomes too much work to swim to shore. Getting where we want to be is about making the swim to shore (where God waits for us) more rewarding than the surrender of continuing to go with the flow. Make your list. Don't cast blame. Own the reasons why you have not pursued the Creator's Intent. It might be painful or sad, but the act will set you free.

IT'S NOT JUST BELIEFS

When you make your list, you will probably notice that many of the reasons that you got off course from the life that you had in mind are related to your beliefs. Remember, beliefs are your thermostat; they will automatically return you to the level you've unconsciously chosen until you change them. If your list is filled with statements like, "I never thought I was smart enough to go to college," then it's likely that you have sabotaged yourself with a set of faulty beliefs. To put it another way, you've been steering your boat using a bad map and it's led you to the rocks.

However, it's not just beliefs that lead us away from the Creator's Intent and toward a life that we don't even recognize. There are other factors at work. Now, this doesn't mean you're not responsible for the impact that these other factors have on your life; you are. Something extremely important I learned about controlling my life's direction was this:

You are responsible for who and what you let into your life and how much power you grant them over you.

In other words, once you're an adult with your own mind, no person, government, or other authority can control the course of your life unless you grant them the power to do so. We choose what we give power to. We can choose to give power to the things that tear us down, or we can give power to the things that lift us up.

So, apart from your beliefs, what else in your life has sidetracked your dreams? Take out your journal and explore these three most common enemies, answering the questions truthfully. It may be difficult and even painful to dig so deeply within your self. Remember to go at your own pace, and be compassionate and forgiving as you work through any challenging experiences or emotional wounds.

1. **The wrong people.** The influence of people from our past or present can be one of the biggest reasons that we don't move toward the destiny that God has already delegated to us. Whether we're the victims of neglectful or abusive parents, teachers who told us that there was something wrong with us because we couldn't sit still in class, bosses who kept us from advancing in our careers, or friends with low goals—we all encounter some people who harm us or hold us back for reasons of their own. What kind of people have you let into your life over the years, and what power have you granted them?

   Also, be mindful of the person who tempts you into a lifestyle that ultimately harms you. This is the person who can influence you to commit acts that go against your personal moral compass—lying to your spouse, cheating on your taxes, sabotaging someone at work, taking drugs, engaging in criminal activities, etc. This kind of person is dangerous because we see them as a friend, and we generally like them. Having healthy relationships is important because we tend to be as addicted to relationships as we are to any chemicals like alcohol or drugs. We desire friendship, camaraderie, and acceptance—in fact, we need them. So vet the people in your social circle regularly, and don't give unhealthy relationships and people any power over your life.

   Rather than allow negative or destructive people to influence you, instead focus on the people in your life who uplift you, support you, inspire you, and believe that you can do great things. Don't turn away positive, empowering people just because they hold views that you don't agree with or because you don't feel worthy of their friendship or help. We all have room in our lives for more unconditional support and belief.

2. **Fears.** There are reasonable fears in this life, such as the fear of poverty and crime, the fear of being drawn into a destructive lifestyle, and even the fear of failing or dying. Some fears are strong, useful warning signs that can help us remain on the righteous path. However, most of our fears about who we are and what we can do are baseless.

Fear is a prison. Fear lies at the heart of many of the reasons that we don't do the things we set out to do. Why is it common to set goals and then not follow through? Because we fear change or the unknown. Fear is the core of anxiety, depression, panic, and paralysis. We fear being wrong. We fear failure, even after we've seen again and again that failure is necessary for success. We fear the disapproval of others. But ask yourself, Is your fear rational? Is it based on real consequences that might happen or on unrealistic fears about what will probably not happen?

Remember this acronym for the word FEAR: False Evidence Appearing Real. Fear distorts reality and takes us farther away from God. When you shine a light on your fears, you will usually find that they are unfounded and fall apart easily. So, what are some fears that have stood in your way, and why have you given them power?

3. **Outdated, blindly followed traditions and rules.** Now, I'm not disrespecting traditions like going to church on Sundays or getting together with family for Christmas. Some traditions are good. Those are the traditions that connect and strengthen us. But some traditions and rules do nothing but limit us. Those kinds of traditions and rules often mask inflexible thinking—in fact, they are

often a substitute for thinking; they keep things as they are so that nobody has to feel the discomfort of change. Outdated traditions and rules make detractors say things like, "We just don't do things that way," or "No one else in this family has ever done that . . ." Many "we always" or "we never" phrases that infect your life are probably limiting what you can accomplish if you never question them and instead blindly follow them.

Jesus Himself violated many of the hidebound traditions and rules of His time in order to convey His message of peace and salvation to the people. He consorted with prostitutes, lepers, and those considered social outcasts in that age. He challenged the money changers at the temple. He preached that the meek are the peacemakers, not the warmongers, and that they would inherit the earth. It was precisely because Jesus refused to be bound by the narrow social conventions of His time that His words had the power to change the world.

Why do you follow traditions and rules in your life? Do you do so blindly? Usually, it's because breaking the rules means disapproval or punishment. You might be disowned by your family, who does not approve of your political beliefs. You might be demoted by a boss who does not like it when employees come up with their own ideas, even when those ideas are better than the established methods. So you must ask yourself: Is it worth it for you to challenge these traditions and rules to progress toward your life's goals? Will the people who get angry with you get over it? If they don't, can you live with that? Not all people can be passengers on your sailboat to your far horizon. You must leave some of them behind.

Ask yourself what price you are willing to pay to strip the power from the traditions and rules that hold you back.

If you realize that an old tradition has become a barrier toward your Creator's Intent, it should be replaced with newer ones that serve the direction of your life and intentions. I, for one, understand how important support is when you decide to start a new custom. You may consider accountability or guidance from friends or professionals to help you filter through the journey of transforming your traditions. In a healthy way, traditions honor legacy, bond relationships, and bind us to a useful identity. Or they can render us irrelevant and bind us to a past action or pattern of thinking that we should actively be releasing ourselves from. Progress requires a shift in a new direction, and seeking guidance is a wise step.

NAMING IS POWER

The final aspect of taking responsibility for your present and transforming your future is the act of naming. It's an act and principle as old as Adam; Adam named the creatures of the earth and sky, signifying that he *accepted* the dominion and responsibility he had over them.

Naming is power; when you call something into the light and determine its nature, you can ensure it stays in its proper place in your life. Unidentified issues will become fears. We fear the unknown in our lives; mystery magnifies danger and power. But when we can name our problem areas, issues, losses, or failures—we have taken the first step toward diminishing the effects of fear. Sometimes we can even make our fears ridiculous and laughable. Wouldn't you love to laugh and have joy about your future again instead of fear?

Breaking It Down: Lead With Your Pivot

To lead with your pivot, you need to learn and bring to light your true self by tapping into the power of naming. Answer these four sets of questions in your journal:

1. What about your life today do you ache to change? Inspect your life for any major patterns or habits that you would like to improve upon: anger patterns, flight versus fight patterns, tendency to overspend, depression, negativity, smoking, cursing, etc. What have you noticed in your life that amount to root problems that you would like to change?

2. How do you want your future to be different from your life today? What does it look like? If you could see yourself in one year, three years, five years, what would you want to be different? What behaviors or conditions do you want to see operating as your new normal? Managing under a balanced budget? Healthier communication with a spouse or child? A different job? This is a place where you should set goals according to the Creator's Intent. It would be unwise to set a goal haphazardly, but set these goals in a way that serves your desires and natural gifts; aim your goals toward the place that accentuates your best parts.

3. What is right about your life today that you would like to keep as it is? If you think about it, everything isn't bad; in fact, you actually have a lot of good qualities working in you. What are those? Which qualities and things in your life can you build on? Do you have a strong family unit that is supportive and helpful? Are you well educated? Are you emotionally supported and strong? Do you love what you do? It's important that when you make decisions you determine how they will affect what is good in your life. Build on what is good and ensure its place in your life by recognizing and affirming its presence in your future. As I mentioned before, all traditions are not bad, and certain things that you identify and name should be preserved for future generations to enjoy. As King David named his enemies, he also named his friends and allies for his successor and son (I Kings 2:5–8). Some parts of your journey should be preserved, protected, and shared. In your naming process, identify what is good so you can manage and secure its place in your life.

4. What must you do differently in order to change what needs to change or transform what should transform? Again, change and transformation are not easy. But with every pivot you make, wise direction is needed. If you are uncertain what to do next, talk to someone. Find an expert or a person with experience that you trust and respect; he or she may offer guidance as to what your next practical steps could be. You do not have to figure out your life on your own. While you must participate in it, there are great tools and people who can serve you well and provide the guidance you need to ensure you are heading in the direction that brings peace to your soul and helps you find true harmony with the will of God.

At a Glance: Leading With Your Pivot

1.   Do not just make a change; make the *right* change.
2.   Be responsible. A key dimension to moving to that pivot point and sticking with it is how we take responsibility for our past, present, and future decisions. It does not matter who is right or wrong; even if someone else did the damage, you must accept responsibility for who or what you've allowed into your life. Accept it, forgive yourself, and pivot.
3.   You must participate in the events of your life in order for the Creator's Intent to be fully expressed in you. An unwilling participant will never reap the rewards of congruence. No burying your head in the sand. Get up and participate in your change!
4.   If you have the capacity to make a poor choice, you have the ability to make a wise one; it's the same ability, just a different choice.
5.   Own your faults. You will discover your dream only after you face the mistakes you've made in your past.

Chapter 4: Discover Your Virtues and Calling

"We're all called. If you're here breathing, you have a contribution to make to our human community. The real work of your life is to figure out your function—your part in the whole—as soon as possible, and then get about the business of fulfilling it as only you can."

—Oprah Winfrey

I was a Midwestern, lower-middle-class kid, and I grew up in a neighborhood where money was scarce but dreams and imagination were plentiful. We all dreamed big—being doctors, lawyers, and professional athletes. For most of the kids in our neighborhood, the natural way to hit it big was to play sports. My sport of choice was football. From my earliest memories, I imagined myself playing in the NFL and being the next Tony Dorsett, the star running back for the Dallas Cowboys in the 1970s and 1980s.

I'm not really sure what drew me to football, because I was a pretty small kid. I also had asthma, so running and playing in the dirt and grass was difficult. My father never let me play organized football, so the rest of the kids always picked me last at the schoolyard because they didn't know if I could play well or not. But there was something about the competition, the physical nature of the game, and the camaraderie of the team that drew me to the sport. It was also a complicated game that I understood instinctively, so much of the athletic portion came to me with relative ease. Football is a thinking person's sport. Contrary to public perceptions, it's a lot more than just a pile of guys knocking one another down and getting up again. If that were the case, I probably wouldn't have lasted as long as I did. The game employs sophisticated strategies that require more precision and execution as you get to higher levels. The game is as much about hand and hip placement, footwork, angles, and field thirds or quarters as it is about brute strength and speed. The difference between the college game and the professional game is like the difference between checkers and chess—same board, different game.

But for some reason, I understood the intricacies of the game of football at an early age. I could do more than just name players and records; I could name offenses, see weaknesses in defensive positions, grasp positional techniques, and so on long before I was formally taught. Football was, and is, in my opinion, the most beautiful team sport of them all. I know now that the reason I was such a football prodigy was that it was part of my Creator's Intent, but back then I just reveled in having a natural gift and figured that's all it was.

At Hazelwood East High School in St. Louis, a high school that was known for producing football stars, I wasn't surprised that I became a good player. I had a quiet confidence inside of me that told me I could do it. Plus, we trained like champions. All summer and all season long we trained and practiced hard. The atmosphere of my high school football team was designed for competition; it was a locker room loaded with guys who played for scholarships, because most of us could not have gone to college without athletic scholarships. We rarely played for fun; fun was a by-product of winning. We were trained that way, so we won a lot. Therefore it was fun.

At the University of Wisconsin, my commitment to the game was the same. In fact, college football demanded even more time and dedication, because the competition was better and the stakes were higher. Technique details mattered more in college than in high school, and also the business element entered our landscape. Now there was television revenue, coaches who needed to win, huge audiences, and massive booster dollars involved, and all of this increased the pressure to perform. Of course, there were rewards. From getting the largest slice of pizza in the lunch line to the first-class treatments in nearly every area of life, being an elite college athlete had its privileges. We played hard and partied like rock stars. So it was easy to lose perspective with the adulation, crowds, national exposure, and stroked egos. In fact, it was easy to *want* to lose yourself in the lifestyle. College football required such a commitment that you had little time to explore other life pursuits, which is not to be confused with having time to get a degree. I had no time to really explore myself and who I was intrinsically, because school and sports detracted from that journey, and more often than I'd like to admit, school got the shorter end of my stick.

Interestingly enough, when I was in college I picked up an intense love for reading. I learned to enjoy learning in a way I could never enjoy football. It was an emotional break from playing and practicing. But by the time I mastered balancing school and sports, I realized I was good enough to play in the NFL. Since I was close to completing my degree, I thought it was best to focus on achieving my lifelong dream of playing professional football. During my final semester of college, I pretty much shunned class in favor of full-time training. I was so close to the dream that I could feel it! But I never saw it as anything bigger than reaching a goal, *my* lifelong goal.

It was such an exciting time that everyone near me got completely wrapped up in helping me reach this goal. As a result, we just about forgot everything else except football. My eating habits, sleeping habits, recreational habits, workout regimen, study habits (or lack thereof)—everything I did was dictated by football. Before long I was wrapped in the cocoon of a ballplayer trying to reach his dream. Well-intentioned people reminded me that pro-football was only a temporary job at best; the average career lasts three years, etc. But like most young people, I didn't listen. I was immortal and invincible. "Get my degree so I'd have something to fall back on? Why? I was going to play fifteen years in the NFL, for Christ's sake!" Or, so I wished, like most budding athletes.

Incidentally, I finally did get my degree. After I got selected in the NFL draft I managed to get back to school in time to finish enough credits and earn my degree in English literature later that summer. But it was my football career that was foremost in my mind.

What football taught me about life is priceless: sportsmanship, teamwork, deference, trust, believing in a bigger plan and vision than just your own. It was the instrument that God used to teach me about purpose, destiny, and functionality, and it allowed me to perform before captive audiences and bring families and communities together. For that season of my life, football was more than just my job or lifelong dream; it was the stage for my calling. Football was the platform that gave me the most opportunity to express the inherent virtues inside of me.

We will now look closely at the two spiritual pillars that will give you the power to fully discover the Creator's Intent for you—*virtue* and *calling*. These two pillars will lay the foundation for discovering your true self and the life you're meant to be living.

YOUR VIRTUES

Finding your true self and the meaning of your life is not as easy as reading a book or taking a test. Discovering the nature of who you are meant to be requires authentic self-inspection and a deep, constant connection to God. I have often wondered if our increased disconnection from God and things Divine is the primary reason why so many seem to wander aimlessly through life. If we separate ourselves from God intentionally, insisting that we exist separate from God—that we are outside of Him—how will we find congruence and receive meaning that satisfies the deeper parts of our humanity, our souls?

While we are not God, we do share in the "divine nature" (II Peter 1:4). We are the expression of God's mind pressed out into the world. God is within us as we share in His prerogatives through congruence. Imagine if everyone in the world could realize and embrace that truth! Society would wander less and find more concrete purpose if we meaningfully reconnected with God. He already knows the journey and the destination for each of our lives.

Consider this statement God made to Jeremiah: "Before I formed you in the womb I knew you; before you were born I sanctified you; I ordained you a prophet to the nations" (Jeremiah 1:5). This statement hits at the heart of purpose, destiny, and significance. It should inspire anyone who feels lost, aimless, and hopeless. It's a powerful, thrilling statement with a wider purpose. God is operating in your life right now.

God knew intimate details about Jeremiah's abilities, capabilities, proclivities, and shortcomings that made him a unique man. More important, God knew these things *before* Jeremiah was formed in the womb—before he was even born! God had a destiny in mind for Jeremiah since the beginning of Creation—to be a prophet to the nations was God's Creative Intent for Jeremiah—his temperament, spiritual and natural gifts, and life experiences pointed to that end. So, logically, God has also had a destiny in mind for *you* since the Creation—because you are part of that Creation!

Can you imagine that? Each of us has always been a part of God's creative imagination, and at birth we were released into a body to play our role in carrying out God's plan for the world. God had His original design planned before Jeremiah had made any decisions about his life.

However, the ultimate choice *became* Jeremiah's: either to cooperate with Heaven's intentions for him and become a prophet to the nations for God, or to act according to his own will and miss this glorious destiny. That's the choice we all face: is it going to be God's will or our own?

Jeremiah's decision to align himself with God, though it did not shield him from all of life's ills, provided him with a tremendous sense of purpose and significance, which is the payment that we all desire from life. The same decision and choice goes for you and me. God knows you better than you do. He possesses what you are searching for—your creative intent. He is the perfect place to begin to learn about your life and purpose. There is an intricate, detailed plan for every part of your life that He cannot wait to share with you. He wants your commitment to discovering your *virtues*. Yes, your virtues.

What is a virtue? Virtues are the most essential element to finding one's Creator's Intent:

God places the DNA of your purpose in your personal virtues.

As DNA is the blueprint for one's genetic expression, so are your virtues the blueprint for your purpose. Whether realized or not, you have been expressing your virtues practically your entire life in some form or fashion. A virtue is *not* a job or a specific kind of action one performs, though a virtue needs an action or job to allow it to be expressed.

Your virtues will manifest your most natural and innate self; it is your set of qualities and Divine merits that yearn to come out. It is not an action but the excellence offered to the world because of the action. The excellence that is you. Your virtues are preprogrammed in your heart and psyche by God. You will desire to express your virtues, you will want to share them with the world, and you will feel amazingly significant when you recognize them and release them daily.

YOUR CALLING

When Jesus was only twelve years old, He was acutely aware of the direction of His life, even if He didn't yet know the specifics. Millions of dollars in tuition money and years of college go to waste every year because we are taught to acquire knowledge before we discover what we need to know—before we discover the direction our lives are supposed to take. It's the equivalent of jumping into your car and driving for an hour before you know a destination. Your life pattern bears the imprint of the virtues God wants you to use, and your calling guides you toward them.

Instead of following a path laid down by someone else, God wants you to discover and follow your *calling*. The ancient Greeks understood a calling to be a type of Divine invitation into a destiny:

> *Your calling is simply the pull from God on your heart and conscience for you to express your virtues consistently to the benefit of yourself and others.*

A calling isn't just your job, it is what your job allows you to pursue and perform regularly. It's the best and highest use of your virtues, expressed through your mind, talent, skills, passion, energy, and faith. The industry of football allowed me to pursue the calling of my life to motivate, inspire, educate, and entertain. Football was the vehicle that allowed me to perform these virtues regularly. Now, being a pastor serves the same purpose football did fifteen years ago.

Some things to know about your calling:

- It is not a possession or a job; it is a beckoning toward the place of your highest use on this Earth and will require you to employ your natural and spiritual skills.

- It is not given to you by anyone of this world, nor can it be taught to you by anyone.
- It is a divinely inspired utterance that leads and requires you to follow it if it will be of any use to you.
- It can be recognized through self-assessment, or by people closely connected to your life patterns.

Discovering your calling will lead you, inevitably, to operating in your virtues. Some of us are called to be ministers, while others are called to be lawyers; and while the job is not the calling, the job is the environment that allows you to fully express your virtues, thus answering the call on your life. Often, people are called to paths that seem contrary to what we are supposed to want—medical school grads called to driving trucks, young women called to the military, retired pro-athletes called to teaching high school. Sometimes we're drawn to what appears to make no sense or doesn't fit with the life that we or our families have planned out so meticulously for ourselves. So we resist. We fight the pull of our calling and continue in occupations that make us miserable. We deny God and try to ignore the virtues that keep appearing again and again. It's no wonder so many millions of people are unhappy!

You are meant to discover both your virtues and your calling and to follow them to greater joy, achievement, and meaning. God has laid down clues throughout your life designed to lead you to them. Scripture says, "For there is nothing hidden which will not be revealed, nor has anything been keep secret but that it should come to light" (Mark 4:22). God is not trying to hide any of this from us.

HOW ARE YOU BENT?

Another spiritual phenomenon you must explore and acknowledge is that everyone has a natural *bend* to their life, a common pattern of their likes, dislikes, optimal environments, and compassions. Have you noticed that there's a bend to the way your life has progressed? By bend I mean your natural inclinations, attractions, and the actions that you bend toward. You are not taught these, only trained and encouraged to honor or resist them. If you have resisted the natural bend in your life, you probably already know the frustration of resisting.

If you have never been taught to acknowledge them, I am certain that you've experienced unexplainable dissatisfactions, discontents associated with not being able to find congruence with this natural bend. I see the signs of it all the time. You can't imagine how many people I have counseled who are unhappy in the career they've spent many years pursuing. Often, they listened to pressure from family or to the desire for money instead of the patterns of their bend, and now they are beginning to despair, feeling that they have wasted years of their lives. It doesn't have to be this way.

A part of finding congruence with the Creator is finding agreement with your natural bend. A true calling will always draw you toward this natural curve. It is important not to let pressure from society, industry, or the well-intentioned teachings of leaders compel you to "unbend" this natural flow toward your calling. I would love to see more parents be conscious about noticing this bend in their children. Ideally, I would like to see them less focused on sending their children to universities that cost thousands of dollars without understanding the nature of true education.

"Education" is from two Latin words, *educare* and *educere*. The first means "to train or rear" as one would a child. However, the second, *educere*, means "to draw out," suggesting that to educate is to draw out that which is already within. Before we compel our children to spend years at a university, we should determine that it will "draw out" their innate virtues and Divine callings and train them so they may contribute to the world in a productive and congruent way. We should train our children toward their natural bend and encourage openness toward releasing it into the world. This applies not only to our children but to ourselves as well. What are you bent toward? Have you allowed it to be drawn out of you? Are you operating according to your inherent virtues?

If you feel exhausted by how you spend your days, certain that life should be something more, feeling that there's something better out there waiting for you if only you could find it, guess what? There is! What you're feeling is the natural consequence of fighting your way uphill through life against God's will and the way you are bent. You can fight and trudge and go your own way, but why would you do that? Why would you ignore your virtues and deny your calling when they will make your life so much richer and bring you closer to God?

So the question is, how are you bent? Your life has given you clear indicators. You have been walking along your natural bend for most of your life. Your virtues, behaviors, and desires have always guided you toward the outcomes that serve God's underlying purpose. A quiet part of you knows that you were born to walk in concert with the Creator's Intent, and He's always steering you toward your calling, even if your conscious mind takes the wheel and steers in the other direction. Whether you are playing basketball at the park as a teenager or sitting in a boardroom as an adult, your virtues and outcomes do not change; the situation and circumstances might, but what you know and feel is right for you never changes. Search for the patterns.

As a twelve-year-old boy, Jesus harbored an inner desire to reconcile, rescue, and restore lives. One day, He stayed behind on a family trip so that He could dialogue with others whose mission was similar (Luke 2:41–52). By the time Jesus was a thirty-year-old adult, not much had changed about Him. Many years had passed, but His virtues and calling were the same. The mission to proclaim the Good News, set free the oppressed, and save humankind remain in line with what He always wanted, even as a child. He was so confident that He was walking in God's dream and living the Creator's Intent that He told everyone that God's plan for Him was the reason He had been sent to Earth (Luke 4:18).

Do you know the reason you were sent? Have you found a sense of what God wants to do with your life? Search your heart and you will begin to rediscover what God already knows.

A Calling Means a Caller

You can't have a calling without a caller. That's why people who have found how to express the intent of God talk about being "called" to their work. They know that the Divine has reached out and placed His hand on them. If you sense a call, what do you need to do in order to answer?

For those whose faith is flagging after years of unmet needs and unfulfilled dreams, this realization can serve as a needed wake-up call. Simply put, the existence of a calling proves that a caller is really out there and really does beckon. The desire for you to answer your needs to create, nurture, or organize is not coded into your DNA naturally or by chance. It is coded there intentionally and purposefully. When time meets proper circumstance, the caller summons that which is imbedded deeply inside of us, that which has been primed to be expressed. Ignoring this brings frustrations. Answering brings peace and meaning.

The only way that a calling to specific purposes can be placed into the mind of a human being is by *another mind*. Parents don't always do it; there are endless stories about parents who try to talk their children out of chasing after their dreams. That's the source of that terrible phrase about having something to "fall back on." It assumes that you will fail, and when you do, you'll need a soft landing place. But succeeding at your dream doesn't have to be as uncertain as winning the lottery. If parents encourage children toward their natural bend, allow for the kind of education that trains their virtues and teaches them to acknowledge their calling, the uncertainty of risk-taking becomes significantly minimized.

Callings are much too specific to be chance. The calling is one of the best pieces of proof that faith is not wasted. Even better, your calling is God's ultimate show of faith in *you*. You have been given the freedom to fall forward, knowing that He will be there to catch you but trusting that you will not fail. He gifts you with your virtues and calling, believing that you are sufficient to bring them to fruition.

You need to discover your virtues and calling, and let them take you where they will. Most of us already have an idea of what we're really good at, but many of us resist the pull of our calling. Callings are not practical, we're told. They're foolish. They're not right for us because of our gender, religion, or background. So we fight what we should surrender to. Instead, start paying attention to where your virtues and calling are trying to lead you.

Pinpoint Your Virtues and Calling

The first step toward discovering your virtues is to complete a simple statement. Write this statement out in your journal:

- I have always been a person who _____
  _____.

How can this statement transform how you see yourself? When you acknowledge who you have always been, you acknowledge your place in the mind of God. You begin to see that a great destiny has always been waiting for you to claim it. That's a profound, thrilling revelation.

How do you begin to fill in that blank space? You do it by looking at your past and present. Inspect your history and connect that thread to today, until it weaves a clear picture. Ask yourself and then write down the answers to these questions:

- What innate qualities—kindness, courage, determination, faith, creativity, vigor, etc.—have consistently enriched and elevated me and the people around me?
- What do I do today that brings me great joy and a sense of purpose?
- How are those innate qualities and joyful, purposeful actions linked? What do they have in common?

When you can answer those questions, you will have identified the pattern you have followed your whole life—possibly without knowing it—and you should be ready to complete your virtue statement. Remember, a virtue is not a job or action but the essence of who you are, so your completed statement might look like one of these:

- I have always been a person who inspired others to surpass their limits.
- I have always been a person who could make others laugh even in the darkest times.
- I have always been a person who people instinctively trust.

If your beliefs are the foundation of transformation, then your virtues are the tool that you will use to bring about that transformation. Your life is built on how you express these virtues. Your virtues determine who you will become when you align with the Creator's Intent. If you're a healer, you might become a nurse, doctor, caregiver, or therapist. If you're highly interpersonal, particularly with children, you might become a teacher or family therapist. If you enjoy creating, perhaps you could be an artist, chef, or designer. Get the picture? The virtue isn't the job; it's the essence of the activity. Your virtues are your fundamental desires that can only be expressed through an action.

God wants each of us to know our virtues and His vision for us. Though it feels far away, it's not meant to be a secret but to be discovered and shared. This is why self-examination is so important. In any act of exploration, the explorer becomes as acquainted with the terrain as possible to optimize his chances of discovery. Your journey to your own personal transformation will not only reveal who you are in your innermost heart but will set you on a journey through the mind and heart of God. Being self-aware will lead you to the discovery of your virtues and your true self.

If you are ready for the journey, here is a simple prayer you can recite:

Father, I believe that you know all of the details concerning my life. I also believe that You want me to know them so I can live a life full of meaning and one that pleases You. Please share Your thoughts with me through events, associations, my history, and Your Word, so I can know who You see me to be.

Amen.

BREAKING IT DOWN: VIRTUES AND CALLING

To further explore your virtues and calling, ask these probing questions and write down your answers in your journal:

- What are your natural gifts?
- When you use your natural gifts positively, what are the results and experiences? (More joy, more education, more clarity, more beauty, more self-worth, encouragement to chase your dreams, etc.)
- What issues or needs keep grabbing your attention? (Injustices, clutter, lack of clarity, poverty, lack of educa-

tion, spiritual ignorance, etc.)
- What virtues are you expressing that make you feel in "flow," like there's no effort?
- Who are the people who receive the most from you when you exercise your gifts?
- What makes you feel divinely inspired?

The answers to these questions are certain to contain information about your virtues and calling. You may discover that the path of your life—the dream that you and God share—has been right before you all along. Follow your virtues and discover the calling that will transform your future.

AT A GLANCE: DISCOVERING YOUR VIRTUES AND CALLING

1. It's important to discover both your virtues and answer your calling.
2. Virtues are the most essential element to finding your Creator's Intent. They are the blueprint of your purpose.
3. You have expressed your virtues your entire life in some fashion or form. They come forth in every season, in everything, and share a common thread from childhood until now. Are you still operating in them or have you allowed life to get you off track?
4. A calling is the Divine beckoning of God to use your virtues. The weight of purpose will lead you to find ways to express your virtues to the world.
5. Your life has a natural bend toward inclinations and actions. Notice and honor them.

Chapter 5: Take Off Your Favorite Shirt

"There are risks and costs to action. But they are far less than the long-range risks of comfortable inaction."

—John F. Kennedy

"Faith to faith" is how Paul the Apostle describes the journey from one act of faith to another act of faith where God's intent is revealed in our lives (Romans 1:17). With every act and leap of your faith, another aspect of divine provision is revealed that you otherwise would not have experienced had you remained in your comfortable place. However, you must make up your mind to move and take that first leap.

Retiring from the NFL wasn't an easy decision by any stretch. Football had been my life ever since I was a child. After eight years of playing with the San Diego Chargers, they released me, and I took the summer off. There were a few different teams calling to inquire about my services, and I felt that if I got healthy enough to play, perhaps I would give it another shot and get a few more years in. I did try to give it another shot by meeting with the Tampa Bay Buccaneers. And I flew down to Florida and had a reasonably good workout with the

Buccaneers. The team needed a running back, and we seemed to be a good match.

However, on the flight back to California, I got the feeling that I wasn't going to get a call back from Tampa—not because I wasn't a good fit for their team but because, as I had felt all summer, God perhaps had something else for me to do. This feeling was extremely conflicting; for the last fifteen years of my life, football was all I had done. What would I do with myself now? Football had given me a purpose, the tools to perform it, a support group that had the same goals as me, and a delightful salary.

For as long as I could remember, my days had been scripted from six in the morning until six at night, and sometimes longer. During the season, I could tell you where I would be, almost to the minute, from Monday through Friday. If I wasn't watching game film, I would be in meetings. If I wasn't in meetings, I would be doing on-field drills, at practice, or working out in the gym. While the team worked extremely hard, the regimented schedule took all the guesswork out of life. When it came to my time, I didn't have to think for myself. It was comfortable and normal to be on automatic, life was predictable, and there was no need to explore any other aspects of my life.

When I begin to sense that God wanted me to move into ministry and trust Him with the next season of my life, I did not initially embrace it. When Tampa decided to go in a different direction, I immediately told my agent to pursue the other calls we had gotten. Even though by then my heart was pointed more toward ministry than football, I automatically reached for my "old favorite shirt." Unfortunately (or fortunately) for my NFL career, those doors were closed to me and I was forced to either pursue what had been changing in my heart, or put my life on hold and wait for one of those doors to open. Through much prayer, Scripture searching, and wise counsel from loved ones and friends, I decided that moving on with my life was the best option.

But it certainly was not the easiest. At times I felt lost in the "real world." Football had been my identity for years, but I had been evicted from my comfort zone and cast into a world without the regimentation that I had become used to. Now it was necessary for me to develop a new sense of self separate from catching and carrying footballs. Though I knew I had other gifts, I had ignored them for years. After all, why would I need them when football was my life? It was a shortsighted attitude that I was now called on to correct—pronto!

In the early months of my retirement, I figured that I would either become a sports announcer or try to move into upper management. However, while those are noble occupations, God was pointing my heart in a different direction that was more in tune with who He thought me to be. Eventually, I hunkered down and said to myself and to God, "If the past me is not what You want, then let's begin the journey of finding who I am supposed to be today." I was beginning to realize that who you used to be can be an enemy to who you want to become. Moving forward often results in losing people, including your former self.

Shortly after praying that prayer, things changed—and boy, did they change! You cannot imagine how many opportunities I had to reject so that I could accept my new future. The cost was enormous. Saying no to yesterday also meant saying good-bye to some well-intentioned people who would not or could not share the journey into this new season of my life. Agents, managers, trainers, and nutritionists—I had to leave behind some amazing people who had invested in my life in wonderful ways.

All in all, saying good-bye to my past was not as simple as I had hoped. It never is. The past has a purchase on us. Though you might separate from the past, you are not detached from the memories, impulses, or desires. Those were a type of cross for me to bear. I still had a passion for football and rich memories of teammates and games. And there were times I was overcome with regret about my decision.

Initially, I did not give everything to the ministry. I kept one foot in each world, resisting God's command for me to let go of my past and embrace my new future. I did some sports announcing while at the same time serving as a youth pastor. Unfortunately, broadcasting did not bring me the joy I assumed it would bring, and it paled miserably in comparison to being on the field. I still wasn't happy or satisfied, but I remained fearful of letting go completely.

However, with every day that passed, I released a little more of my football world. At the same time, I exercised my faith a bit more. Slowly, I came into congruence with what God was doing with my life. My first commitment was to becoming a senior pastor. As time went on, I realized that everything I did from that point on must flow from the river of ministry. Preaching, teaching, coaching, book writing, seminars, even football—they all had to serve my ministry. I was all in with my new purpose, and I finally found certainty and joy.

After ten more years, God led me back to football—this time not as an announcer or coach, but as the chaplain for the San Diego Chargers. I am able to continue to walk in God's intent for my life in a different environment while still being involved in the sport that I love. Wonderful and mysterious are the paths we walk in God, and when we have faith, the results are incredible.

Your Favorite Shirt

In professional football, when the quarterback lines up behind the center to take the snap and sees that the play he called is not lining up the way he would like—maybe the defense is planning to blitz, for example—he'll often call an "audible." He'll shout new signals to his players, telling them that the play is changing in the moment. An audible is improvisational, leaving the comfort zone of the designed play to try something new. Audibles are risky, but they're also necessary.

Sometimes, the only way that you can achieve success and get the reward that you want is by taking a risk.

In the world of motivational speaking, calling an audible is similar to getting outside of your comfort zone. The comfort zone is a behavioral space where the things you do and even your thoughts fit a routine that reduces your stress and risk. In that space, you feel secure. Anxiety and stress diminish or disappear. It feels good to be in that familiar place. However, the comfort zone can also be a trap. Research has shown that while being in that zone makes you perform at a steady state, being slightly outside of that zone—where you feel a small amount of anxiety and uncertainty—compels you to deliver excellence. In other words, the only thing that is at its absolute best in a comfort zone is comfort itself.

Stepping just outside that area of comfort is the best way to be the best you. When we live in an undercurrent of anxiety and stress, we're compelled to act. Our minds race to come up with solutions. We push our capabilities like never before. We feel smarter, stronger, more alive. That's why so many people become habitual entrepreneurs and constantly start new businesses—the adrenaline rush of uncertainty and challenge is a healthy addiction. It's what sets their souls on fire. How about you? What sets your soul on fire?

Now, calling an audible is not a universal prescription. There are people who do very well with routine and familiarity. It's counterproductive to venture so far out of your comfort zone that you're terrified. But when you're dealing with the task of trying to discover your virtues and calling, being prepared to step outside of your comfort zone is crucial; it's how God takes you to new places. Every step into new, unexplored territory requires you to step away from the old, the familiar. God doesn't want you to be comfortable; He wants you to be ambitious, joyous, filled with purpose, and at peace knowing that your purpose will never guide you to a place you cannot succeed in. Think about Paul the Apostle, traveling endlessly to spread the Good News. People of purpose cannot become comfortable, because comfort leads to complacency, and the fires of passion go out.

Instead of using the well-worn phrase "comfort zone," I prefer to talk about your old "favorite shirt." Have you ever had a favorite article of clothing that was so broken in and perfectly fitted it just made you feel good to put it on? My friend Tom does. It looks good on him: it tucks well, fits well around his shoulders, and goes with virtually anything he puts on. It's his go-to shirt when he needs to feel sharp and confident. Almost without thinking, he grabs this shirt for important meetings and when he wants to look good socially. He probably wears this shirt three times as often as any other shirt in his closet (and he's got some nice shirts in there).

But, in a way, the shirt is holding Tom hostage. His confidence and self-assurance are connected to wearing it. Even if the shirt is dirty, he will take it out of the hamper, iron it, and make it work. The shirt makes him feel safe. I think we all have a shirt like that in our closet. If it's not a shirt, it's something else in our lives—places we go, people we trust, books we read, attitudes we default to, beliefs we cling to. Even if they are harmful and unhealthy, we gravitate toward them because they give us a sense of confidence and safety. The trouble is that God did not bring us into this world to be comfortable. He brought us here to strive, build, speak, create, and occupy.

Those who turn out to be society's most successful are the ones who create a healthy tension within themselves between being good at the familiar and stepping into the unknown. This produces the urgency necessary to defeat complacency and, sometimes, create greatness.

Acting in the Creator's Intent means taking off that favorite shirt and stepping into something unfamiliar. It's getting into the zone where intellect, knowledge, and ability are secondary to faith, trust, and sovereign rule. It's where cosmic action produces cosmic results. It's the zone where God makes things happen. This demands courage, but knowing that you're acting according to a Supreme will should give you courage.

Consider the actions of the great Earvin "Magic" Johnson, still considered one of the greatest National Basketball Association (NBA) players in its history. When he retired from the NBA in 1992 due to contracting HIV, he was an NBA champion, a rich man, and world famous; he could have spent the rest of his life living quietly. Instead, he challenged the status quo, came back to basketball, and ended up playing on the Olympic "dream team." He became part owner of the Los Angeles Lakers and now leads the ownership team of the Los Angeles Dodgers and is a major player in the black community, opening franchises such as Starbucks, TGI Fridays, and 24 Hour Fitness centers in areas where other investors wouldn't, like South Central Los Angeles. His life has brought hope to millions of people, but particularly African Americans and those living with HIV, encouraging them to fight on to live awe-inspiring lives. Talk about taking off your favorite shirt!

Those decisions could not have been easy for Magic. He was an athlete, not a real-estate developer, and it was a huge risk to his brand, his finances, and even his health to venture into crime-ridden areas of major cities in order to try and lift them up. He must have felt apprehension, even fear. But he persisted. A man of faith, he drew courage from knowing that this new path was God's calling for him, and even though it was outside his comfort zone, he was confident he would find strength there. His success speaks for itself because his gifts—his resources, opportunities, and courage—were planted on the pathway his calling led him to. So are yours, so do not fear the unknown. When you draw your courage from knowing that you are working in congruence with God's plan, you will find the ability to act on what you have discovered about yourself so far. And you will be able to work wonders!

THE WALK OF FAITH

To do all of this, you need that which is most fundamental: *faith*. The walk of faith is God's intended way for us to walk with Him. It is a requirement. "But without faith, it is impossible to please Him . . ." (Hebrews 11:6). God cannot be satisfied without our faith in motion.

Furthermore, a faith walk is expected: "the just shall live by faith" (Hebrews 10:38). Faith is a necessary and a central element of God's design for you. Without taking risks, which are leaps of faith, we become slaves to the circumstances that make us feel comfortable or, in some cases, uncomfortable. As money is to our natural world, faith is to the spiritual world. The currency for spiritual resources is paid with faith. The more you have of it, the more you will experience the trade-off of extraordinary return. Faith is our assurance that, when we take that comfortable favorite shirt off, God will not leave us naked.

Comfort, as we have seen, can be a blessing or a curse. Comfort is a blessing when it leads you to a place with no worry and your soul is content. However, it can be a curse if being comfortable saps your drive and desire to serve God's calling in your life. Let's take the Children of Israel as an example. For nearly four hundred years the Children of Israel were slaves to the Egyptian kingdom. Their forced labor helped build a massive dynasty in the land of Egypt before God decided that the Israelites should be freed. God used Moses to perform a series of miracles in an effort to convince the Egyptian pharaoh to release them (Exodus 5–11). After ten plagues scourged the land, the pharaoh relented and reluctantly agreed to free the Israelites.

However, after intense consultation with his family and cabinet, the pharaoh reneged on his promise and ordered the Israelites' exodus from Egypt to be halted. The Children of Israel were on the edge of the Red Sea, preparing to enter into a land of freedom, when they got the news that the pharaoh had changed his mind and had sent an army after them to force their return. It was here, at the edge of the Red Sea, that one of the most noted biblical miracles occurred. God sent a strong wind to split the sea apart, so the Children of Israel could walk along the seafloor to get to the other side. When they reached the other side, the pharaoh's army figured it could take the same route, but when they did, God released the waters to drown them all, leaving the Israelites safe.

God proved a mighty hand of deliverance for Israel. You would think that they would be eternally grateful for being set free so miraculously, wouldn't you? Not so fast. After a brief celebration, the Israelites began to notice that there were no houses in the new land; they would have to build them. Also, there were no available foods in the new land; they would have to hunt. Nor was there a set structure they could use to govern themselves; it would have to be created. The realization that God's miracles necessitated their active participation was not easy for them to accept.

This realization made them murmur and complain, saying, "Oh, that we had died by the hand of the Lord in the land of Egypt, when we sat by the pots of meat and when we ate bread to the full! For you have brought us out into this wilderness to kill this whole assembly with hunger" (Exodus 16:3). Because freedom required a different type of responsibility from them, the Israelites saw their freedom as proof of their coming deaths instead of as an opportunity to draw out their gifts, discover their purpose apart from the Egyptians, and test the limits of what God could perform through their lives. They put a negative spin on freedom—and a positive spin on their time in captivity—to the degree that many wistfully said that they preferred the comforts of slavery to the challenge of freedom!

What happened to the Israelite community is what happens to many of us today: we get so comfortable in our bondage that we begin to prefer slavery over authentic freedom because there is a certain level of familiarity and comfort to it. The Children of Israel, like many of us, rationalized their dysfunctional state to be something less than what it really was. Instead of identifying it as dysfunctional, they named it as a place where they had "meat" and "bread." This rationalization was how they had enabled themselves to survive in slavery. Too many of us spend our time trying to make a dysfunctional situation functional—deluding ourselves that everything is fine—when we should be finding the courage to be free and leave it behind. It is God's intent for you to be free from beliefs, circumstances, or situations that hinder you from walking in faith and sharing God's vision for your life.

What chains have you been walking in that you'd prefer to keep on? In what areas of your life have you refused to step out in faith? Are you enslaved by fear? Addiction? Unproductivity? Comfort?

The Children of Israel found a way to make themselves comfortable in their bondage state. They created for themselves a world, at least psychologically, that allowed them to cope and socially maneuver in an environment that was oppressive. That's not an unusual state. Why do people stay in unhealthy relationships when it would be better to leave? Why do people who hate their jobs remain in them for decades rather than seek new employment? It's because for some people, at least in part, even poisonous comfort is safer than the unknown. We as humans fear the unknown, and nothing more than the unknown future. The possible barriers, challenges, even potential success are not guaranteed, and an unknown future is difficult to choose when your current reality feels safe and manageable. Even those of us with an unshakable faith in God can doubt and quake at the idea of dealing with the unknown. But we cannot allow that fear to keep us from our dreams. Our faith in God must be stronger, strong enough to overcome the fear.

The comfort of the familiar for the Children of Israel made them unwilling (not unable) to endure the privations and mystery of the wilderness to which God led them. They were hesitant to pay the price of letting go of what they were used to for the freedom they deeply sought. They allowed their spiritual muscles to become slack and lost the ability to have faith or to believe that God would not forsake them.

TAKING OFF THE OLD SHIRT

When you walk the path toward the Creator's Intent, you must examine what should stay in the past and what can go with you. In my case, what had to stay was an active engagement in the game that solely produced athletic gain. The part of football that I was able to bring with me on my new journey was the aspect of the game that allowed me to freely impart words of wisdom and encouragement toward a sure destiny to everyone who would listen.

This is one of the hardest aspects of walking away from your comfort zone—not looking back or regretting your decision. It's like you're moving out of a beloved house that's crumbling beneath your feet; even though you know it's not the place for you anymore, there are so many good memories that you're tempted to stay. If you can't stay, you want to bring part of that world with you. So you pack your boxes of memorabilia, then go back and grab a few more things that you can't bear to part with. Then a few more. Before you know it, you're carting your entire past with you into your new space. It's time for you to decide on a course of action and prepare to live with the results.

Instead of circling around in indecision and wasting time, it's time to ask yourself some hard questions about where you are on your journey and where you should be. It's time to take out your journal and venture from your comfortable chair and take off that favorite old shirt:

- Are you happy where you are or are you merely content but dulled and bored?
- Do you feel in your heart that life can be more?
- Are you serving God in what you do each day or are you serving yourself?
- Are you serving others in what you do or are you only serving yourself?
- Is this the best you can be or is there something inside you that's untapped and waiting to come out?
- What frightens you about stepping out of your comfortable world?

What the answers to those questions tell you is that it's time to walk in faith, without a net, and let God lead you into a new realm. Then you must decide what to leave behind. Here are some words of wisdom that can help in this process of letting go:

- **Take your time.** Your destiny waited for decades for you to discover it. It will wait for you for a few more weeks or months while you decide what aspects of your old life are too precious to lose. Once you decide to leave certain things behind, they are often impossible to recapture in the same manner, so make sure you're taking with you what's important and what serves God's purpose for your life.

- **Consider people most carefully of all.** People can be (and most likely have been) the most valuable or most damaging forces in your life. The right people will understand your act of faith and support it, even if they do not fully understand it. They will uplift and believe in you and complement the skills you have with their own gifts. The wrong people will doubt and try to dissuade you from making this uncomfortable change, or they will encourage you toward the change they would make. They may resent any successes you might have moving forward. Some will be terrible behavioral influences and tempt you to waste time with relationship dalliances or destructive habits. So consider well with prayer and discernment.

- **You don't necessarily have to change everything.** What you read, movies you see, foods you eat, places you travel, or people in your life don't all have to change in order for you to move on to the next stage of your journey. Some of the pieces of your life are harmless pleasantries and other things are just meant to be permanent. Those permanent things are necessary to keep because they play a valuable role at every stage of your development. Certain people, habits, and learned ethics can be guiding principles in every season of your life or serve as the things that keep us humble. Many things will change, but not everything has to.

- **Watch for signs and clues.** Just as the experiences of your life will reveal the Creator's Intent, they will also show you which people, behaviors, and possessions belong in your new life and which ones don't. Pay particular attention to patterns; patterns reveal arrangements and habits of behavior. Keep your antennas up to determine how you and others respond to a particular pattern, whether helpful and inspiring or sabotaging and unhealthy.

Where are you in your journey? Have you found your ocean into which all of your streams of purpose should flow? It is God's intent that you do. Take off your old shirt—those places, people, and things that you are comfortable in but which hold you back—and step out in faith based on your new understanding of God's intent for your life! Unchain yourself and follow God's call.

Breaking It Down: A Leap of Faith

- What have you discovered about yourself since beginning this book?
- Have you identified the beliefs that have been holding you back? Or the transformation that you want to undergo?
- Have you identified some clues to what your virtues and calling are?

Remember: these things mean *nothing* unless you *act* on them—and we rarely take meaningful action when we are too comfortable. The deeper your faith—the more you rely exclusively on God to avoid falling and to prevent you from getting lost in unfamiliar country—the greater your discoveries will be. When you trust that your provisions will be provided from above and not from your hands alone, you will be able to resist the urge to grab for your old, comfortable favorite shirt again. Instead, you will reach out for the new, exciting challenges that lie ahead.

AT A GLANCE: TAKING OFF YOUR FAVORITE SHIRT

1. Who you were can be an enemy to who you want to become. You do not have to abhor or dislike the person you were, only acknowledge that you must evolve into a wiser, more strategically congruent self.

2. Your past victories and failures can hold you back. Don't allow them to become the force that prevents you from moving forward.

3. The only thing that is at its absolute best in a comfort zone is comfort itself. You need challenges, and you need to participate in a space that stretches your gifts and intellect, which allows you to grow and produce beyond your dreams. Comfort zones don't build dreams; they maintain sleep.

4. God places the gifts that produce resources, opportunities, and the courage to seize them on the pathway toward your purpose. If you follow where God is calling, these things are sure to appear.

5. Faith is the currency of the extraordinary. Spiritual resources require faith. Faith in yourself, but also faith in

the Divine realm, is often overlooked and underutilized. Do not think it strange to summon Heaven for supernatural intervention. And think it even less strange to expect it. It's okay: ask God for it.

6. Bondage requires you carry a burden; freedom requires you carry responsibility. The trade-off to being in control of your life is that you will now be the sole person responsible for it. No one will tell you what to do, but how you envision discipline, effort, research, and fortitude matter. You can forfeit this and be a worker in someone else's vision, or you can carry the weight of responsibility and live out the vision God gave you.

7. "Beds are made; decisions are lived with." Make your decision and prepare to live with the results.

Chapter 6: Look for the Creator's Clues

"All truths are easy to understand once they are discovered; the point is to discover them."

—Galileo

In the first part of *The Book of You*, we focused on an understanding of the meaning of key spiritual principals like transformation, congruence, pivot, virtue, and calling. The purpose of mastering these principles is to help us discover and design our futures around the Creator's Intent, the plan that God has put in place for our lives.

But how are we supposed to figure out God's design—the Creator's Intent—in the midst of all of the people and events taking place in our world? Let's look at the football locker room as an illustration. One of the things that few people realize about professional football is that, along with weight training, perfecting plays, and learning the playbook, at the heart of a good team and player is the habit of intensive game film study. Believe it or not, professional teams collectively spend thousands of hours a week watching and reviewing recordings of past games.

Teams spend an enormous amount of money on film crews that record, edit, and distribute game film within minutes of the action on the field. And everybody watches film—scouts, coaches, and players alike—to look for mistakes, keys to success, patterns, flaws in mechanics or positioning, and anything else that will give the team an advantage in the future. I remember playing the Detroit Lions one year, and from watching film of that team's previous games our scouts picked up a hand signal from one of their coaches on the sideline. It seemed like every time the offense changed a play from a pass to a run, the coach would make an assortment of physical gyrations but ultimately touch his ear. We were uncertain if it was a signal or a nervous response, but we were right nearly the entire first half of the game until they caught on that we'd picked up on the signal. This is how extensive film study is.

A team will watch film of their upcoming opponents, their own games and practice drills, plus teams they are not playing but which use offensive and defensive strategies that are similar to the team they will play! Trust me, by Sunday, your eyes hurt.

The average professional football player spends at least four to five hours each day watching game film with the team. Then he's given more film to watch at home, on airplanes during travel, and in his hotel room. Coaches will watch film well past midnight every night searching for an edge. As you can see, game film is an important aspect and strategy of any team's success. As a team, we are always looking to find clues that will tell us the opponent's tendencies—weaknesses and strengths—helping us strategize for the upcoming game. Knowing those tendencies can give a diligent team a big advantage.

Watching game film is tedious—play, rewind, take notes—it used to make me dizzy sometimes! But from this introspective and reflective repetitive activity, coaches and scouts are able to formulate a master plan for their team's success. In the same way, you can benefit by looking at the past "film" of your life to determine what your game plan should be. Your past holds the key to God's design for your life. He set it up that way and has been placing clues about His intent in your heart and path since the day you were born. When you learn how to see them, they will become clearly visible to you, because they've been there all along!

Let's think about that again for a moment. The clues to what the Creator wants from you and has always intended for you have been all around, impacting your life since before you could remember. In fact, the same clues are present in your life right now, as you are reading this book. Reading this book may itself be a clue as to what God intends for you! Isn't that extraordinary? God designed the world and its experiences to be a map to guide humanity, showing us how we can best express our highest purpose and take our place in God's plan. If you know where and how to look for the clues, then your life does not need be a mystery.

The trouble is, many of us have no idea that God has scattered clues throughout our past and present, and we need guidance to understand. When we're younger, we actively ignore the idea that anyone—even God—exerts influence over our lives. But just as many younger, less experienced football players either don't value film study or don't know how to use it properly, the experienced veteran players are there to help them understand its value and use. Parents, teachers, mentors: our young people need us to help them see the clues God has scattered throughout their lives and guide them toward these clues, because they don't yet know that true success comes when you follow God's path. Hopefully, as we become more mature, we figure out that following God's path doesn't mean that He dictates every step to take, which foods we buy, our clothing choices, or other common sense decisions. Following God's path is becoming aware of what He knows about you—your natural bend, virtues, and calling. Your past can help to offer these clues.

LEARN FROM YOUR PAST

Some people try very hard to forget their past, particularly if theirs was difficult. But I counsel people to do the opposite. You don't have to relive it, but you do have to learn something from it. The past holds clues to the Creator's Intent for you. The history from your childhood up until now has been an unfolding of God's intentions. It reveals pre-programmed pieces of your psychological makeup, spiritual disposition, and social positioning. These preprogrammed aspects of you never really change. For example, when you're five years old your clue might be nothing more than a deep love for numbers. That's all you can understand as a small child. But with the proper guidance, by the time you reach high school, the clues could become clearer and mature into a love for mathematics. In college that same abiding preprogramming might lead you to a business or science degree. You will start to see patterns that repeat year after year.

When I was in grade and middle school I was crazy for collegiate-style wrestling. John Smith, Kendall Cross, Buddy Lee, and, of course, my own oldest brother, Myron, were among my favorites and it inspired me to join the wrestling team. As much as I enjoyed wrestling my primary concern was not only for my own wins and losses; I got as much enjoyment out of encouraging my teammates to win as I did from winning myself. I realized that what legitimized my ability to push the best out of them, is that they saw me win as well. All I cared about was winning so I could help others win. Then, as I transitioned into high school, my interest in why I played sports turned into a pattern. As I progressed to starring in football, my passion for team and individual success became the tool that I used to constantly improve my performance. By paying close attention to this pattern, I found ways to do what I had always wanted to do: lead and inspire others. Without even realizing it, my focus on teamwork and competition put me on a deeper path and purpose that God wanted me to be on.

Clues to the Creator's Intent that unfold in your past become people, events, and opportunities in your present. That's why it's not just important to read the clues from your past, but it's also critical to understand the clues and signs that appear in your present life from this point forward, because both sets of clues will often share a common thread. Together, they hold the key to the way that you fit into this world and what your greatest contributions can be—your calling or purpose.

I am currently and essentially the nine-year-old wrestler, who wins so he can inspire others to win. The arenas have changed through time, but I'm the same me. It has been this way for my entire life, a thread that weaves through every season of my development and will be a part of my future development. You cannot deny your patterns. They represent your truest self—God's truest intentions.

Start identifying the patterns that have appeared in your life again and again: What do you care about? What's your role in other people's lives? In those patterns, you'll find signs of your Creator's Intent—God's *original thought* about you. It's essential to your life's progress to figure out how to read the mind of God.

God has left clues about His design for you in every experience you've had. Clues that shine bright in the choices you've made, the games you've played, how you played them, the books you were attracted to, the type of people you surrounded yourself with, the burden of your heart, and much more. Like a paleontologist who sees dinosaur bones where the untrained eye only sees rocks, you must be able to look beyond a regular childhood activity or an obsessive hobby to see what else is there.

So when you think about yourself as a child playing baseball on the playground, you may only think about a child having fun. But with your new outlook, you can see something more: a child who loved baseball and was learning how to lead or to fit into the concept of a team.

Perhaps you were drawn to it because it is a game of detail and skill, more cerebral and mechanical than other games, with unspoken rules, and lots of judgment calls. And say you were motivated by the various and specialized positions that both independently and codependently functioned together to make a play happen. From this new perspective, perhaps you'll see that, in those childhood years, you were indeed being guided toward expressing virtues that may in fact have led you to become a professional baseball player, coach, or scout. Or perhaps they pointed to being an astronaut, doctor, or teacher—all opportunities to express the same virtues you expressed as a child on the baseball team, but in different arenas. Learn to study the events, coincidences, passions, and people from your past—to read them like a map—and pick out the subtle hints that were clearly meant to push you in a certain direction through the wild grass, in the direction that God has always had in mind for you.

For an example, look at the life of King David. He was raised in circumstances that could not have been more different from the eventual destiny that awaited him, yet symbols and signs abounded in his life, the most obvious being the battle that he fought against the Philistine champion Goliath. When pleading his case as to why he should be the representative of Israel to battle Goliath, he used his past to map out his future. "But David said to Saul, 'Your servant used to keep his father's sheep, and when a lion or bear came and took a lamb out of the flock, I went out after it and struck it, and delivered this lamb from its mouth; and when it arose against me, I caught it by its beard, and struck and killed it. Your servant has killed both the lion and the bear; and this uncircumcised Philistine will be like one of them . . ." (I Samuel 17:34–36).

David's petition was more than lip service. His pattern had shown him how to be a caretaker, warrior, and protector, and in Israel's most crucial conflict to date, he used the events of his life as the tools to achieve one of the most improbable victories of all time. David, of course, went on to become King of Israel and Judah, not because he defeated Goliath but because his patterns showed his responsible nature, care, initiative, tenacity, and willingness to serve. The throne gave David an opportunity to express his collection of virtues and follow his calling.

Two Perspectives

Your life was intended to move in congruence with a path designed by God. People often want to know, "Is there really a plan?" When terrible things happen, when the best plans fall short and leave us in pain—it can seem that God isn't in charge. I assure them that there is a plan, because God thought through our lives and set a plan before we were born.

I have a sister a few years younger than me, and when we were much younger, as her big brother, I used to give her dating advice. I figured I could let her into the mind of a guy, so she could make wise choices for herself during the date. I would share with her boy tips and clues to look out for to determine if the guy was ready to be "the guy" for her.

On a first date, I advised her, after the guy picks you up at the front door, wait until you are walking toward the car and then do these two things:

1. Ask him, "Where are we going and what are we doing?"
2. Look to see if he has to move anything out of the front seat before you sit down.

If he does not have an answer for what the evening entails and if he has to move books, clothes, etc. out of the front seat, he has not properly planned for you. He cannot ensure you a fun and happy evening, because he did not prepare anything fun or happy. So now the potential is for two teenagers to be out and about without a purpose. It's a recipe for trouble, and being a big brother, I didn't want to see my sister deal with any trouble!

Fortunately, God planned for your presence—He planned an entire lifetime for you, including protection, provisions, directives, and blessings. Notice Jeremiah 29:11: "For I know the *plans* I have for you, *plans* to prosper you and not to harm you, *plans* to give you hope and a future" (NIV; emphasis mine). No person is without purpose while they are alive on Earth, because God is a planner. There are no coincidences in your life; God put a plan and a strategy together to ensure your future. This is where personal development and faith come into play, and here are three points to keep in mind as you continue your journey of self-discovery:

1. **Keep God's "big picture" perspective in mind.** As you live each day, be mindful that there are twists and turns that you cannot see, but God can. His Divine omniscient perspective has a vantage point that is all-knowing and all-seeing, taking every option of your life into account as He guides you daily. In the midst of every event of your life, opportunity is present. Even if it takes you a while to see it, do not despair; meaning will reveal itself at the right time.

2. **Develop your virtuous qualities.** Work to develop them all, but be patient. The developmental process of discovery, revelation, and understanding takes time. As the old adage says, "Rome wasn't built in a day," and neither is a new life. It is a marathon, not a sprint. And as you develop your qualities, so will God's plan begin to develop in your life. Practice patience, because worry and anxiety will not speed up the process.

3. **Trust that the major events of your life tell a story.** God never wastes a hurt. He redeems everything. No matter how joyful, successful, traumatic, or painful the major events of your life are, each event will help you unpack the virtues and qualities of your life. Explore them, dissect them, and find meaning in them. One way that I redeem the events in my life (good or bad) is by trying to identify where I was able to express the best of me in the midst of it. Where was my outlook positive? Where did I have a healthy influence on others? When did I display honor and integrity? Was I able to see a bigger picture brewing? During disappointing moments, I do the same. I tell myself that my best me would not have come out if not for this particular event, and I trust that each event, at its least, is serving this purpose of stretching and challenging me.

LEARNING FROM OUR STORIES

Even the most unexpected events of our past will help tell our story. A bit about me: I don't really have friends. By the time I consider someone a friend, they are more like family, and I see them as such. With that being said, my best and closest friend died abruptly in his late thirties from pancreatitis. A father, friend, popular community leader, and otherwise healthy God-fearing man complained of a stomachache on a Thursday, and abruptly, passed away just over a week later.

We supported each other like brothers. He was a fan of me as a player and as a pastor/community leader. To have that kind of deep support was priceless, and you can imagine the emotions and questions I had at his passing. His siblings, family members, and friends struggled to find meaning in his loss. "God always takes the good ones," we said to calm ourselves, but the reality of it was that we were angry, confused, and at a loss to find meaning in his death. His family and greater community did an amazing job holding themselves intact as a unit.

I became somewhat of a spokesperson and eventually was asked to eulogize him at the service. My best friend, who was like family to me, a true brother—how could I muster words, strength, and desire to perform a duty in the midst of my wish to just grieve and cry? After prayer and counsel with the family, I chose to honor my brother by eulogizing and mastering his service. Because he was well loved, and lived so honorably, the outpouring of love and respect was overwhelming. The service became a big deal in numbers and in community attention. And though it was difficult for us all, I'm glad I did my part. I believe it honored his legacy and his family's request, brought peace to the community, and a cathartic release to my heart personally.

Consequently, saying yes in such a difficult time also marked the beginning of a significant shift of ministerial influence for me in the city of San Diego. It was the first time a mass of community members and leaders were able to experience me beyond my being a football player. That day, while honoring my friend, my community and I witnessed God's pivot in my life and my contributions. My first community appointments stemmed from this experience; my first invitation to participate in a meaningful way to address social issues in our city grew from this as well, and to this day many people belong to the City of Hope International Church because they heard me that day, eulogizing my best friend.

Even events that are hurtful, or that you don't understand, are designed to affect your life. It is all working, right now, in some way to make you and the world better. You may feel like you've hit a brick wall or that you're at a dead end in life, but even dead ends give direction. If nothing else, they tell you that you've been going in the wrong direction. God is in control and has been orchestrating your life like a master conductor; you only need to be willing to play your tune when it's your turn—even if it's a melody of grief.

We've been talking about personal choices and involuntary events that have led your life down a very specific path, and I hope that you are able to see that everything that's happened to you will be used as a part of God's intentional purpose. And no, I do not believe that God purposefully orchestrates or creates bad things to happen to us; we do a good enough job ourselves. However, God uses every opportunity to offer His Divine Will in such a way that it can become an asset to our purpose and an unveiling point to our meaning. It's awesome to know that the Divine will not give any circumstance in your life enough power to ruin His original intention. It is our free choice to choose how we will respond to life's events and situations, and it's crucial to remember:

> *God lays down the path that you should walk; life itself brings obstacles, but you must decide how you will respond to the obstacles if they are to be opportunities.*

To put it another way, God is at the wheel of your ship. He is always steering you on a course that will take you home safely. However, as you pull in at each port of call, you decide whether or not to disembark the ship and what to do with your time onshore. Knowing this actually makes it easier to trust God's intent, even when you encounter times in your life that are difficult, painful, or even unfair, because you know that it's not the events that matter but the choices you make in responding to them. Even dark times can shape you in ways that make you stronger, wiser, and more compassionate. Even times of plenty can harm your future if you make poor choices, as the many lottery winners who have wound up in poverty can attest.

You and God are collaborators in your future. You both play your part. As Scripture says in Philippians 2:13, "for it is God who works in you both to will and to do for His good pleasure."

How to See the Clues

You are undeniably gifted. It is important to know how magnificently blessed you have been with God's gifts. Some are gifted in athletics, while others excel naturally in education, the arts, or as caregivers. Natural, seemingly effortless excellence at something is one clue of the Creator's Intent, but there are many others. When a person is unaware of their primary gifts, they are likely to miss possibilities that could bring them great satisfaction. Being aware of your gifts will allow you to remain open to opportunities that will help you to fulfill your dreams.

Understanding and knowing the nature of your innate gifts is one key way of discovering God's design for your life. Too often, people ignore the story that their innate gifts are trying to tell. If you're a natural writer, singer, teacher, or problem solver, God is trying to tell you: "This is a vein you could be operating in." Your gifts make you marketable, usable, and valuable to a world that needs you to express that gift somehow. The world needs you to be an instrument of God, to help bring about His will in shaping the world into the best place it can be. Your destiny is to play an important role in fulfilling God's will.

How can you start looking for the clues in your past and present? Here are some examples of clues and questions to explore in your journal. Take your time and practice being open to what you discover about your Creator's Intent:

- Occupations or causes that you're passionate about, from writing songs to teaching children how to read to computer programming. What are the situations that bring you to these passions? Who are the people who introduce you to them?

- Activities that you're naturally good at that also bring you joy—sports, music, art, cooking, politics, public speaking, problem solving, writing, numbers, you name it.
- Opportunities or events that come out of nowhere or keep recurring in your life, such as repeated chances to speak, teach, or repair things. This is the general public affirming what God has implanted in you.
- Recurring dreams. What need do you see yourself fulfilling? Are you healing suffering and pain, or solving problems? Giving love to those who need it?
- Books or movies you love. What do their topics or messages have in common?
- People who come into your life for no reason. When new people enter your life randomly, it's rarely random. Who are they—artsy, business types, spiritual guides? What do they inspire in you? What do they need and what do they bring you?
- Ideas you can't stop thinking about. What do your ideas have in common?

Do you recall any of these things in your past, including your recent past? Think back and recall how you saw those occurrences then versus how you see them after learning about the Creator's Intent. With your new perspective, can you perceive the pattern? Can you discern where God was trying to lead you with clues, signs, and portents?

One thing I suggest is that in your journal you pay close attention to the clues that may be embedded in your answers, memories, and reflections. Write down events or people from your past that might have been clues to the Creator's Intent, and write down things that come into your awareness from this point on that seem to be clues as well. Over time, you should start to see patterns, and then you'll know:

God is working in your life to guide you to who you were meant to be.

CREATOR'S CLUES EXERCISE

1. Create life segments out of key stretches of time in your life. Examples:

    a) Childhood memories to grade school
    b) Grade school to middle school
    c) High school to college
    d) College to graduation
    e) Graduation to career
    f) Some other significant period, such as getting married or having your first child

2. Answer these questions for each life segment:

    a) What activities gave you the most enjoyment?
    b) Who were the people you remember being closest with?
    c) What most interested you?
    d) What aspect of life seemed to have the most meaning?

3. Take notice of the commonalities between each segment. You will notice that even though the events and faces changed, the types of people you spend your time with and their character won't vary much. You will notice that the way you showed up—dedicated, indifferent, angry, helpful, a leader, a secondary fig-

ure, etc.—on the high school basketball team is likely the same way you showed up at your first job.

4. Answer these questions for each life segment:

   a) Were you more free then or now?
   b) Were you more joyful?
   c) How have you changed?
   d) Was there a point in your life when you started to turn away from what brought you the most joy, meaning, and sense of purpose?

This exercise is meant to give you a bird's-eye view—a God's-eye view—of the arena you should be playing in. We all begin life with a clear connection to God the Creator and His intent for us. We're clear on what we want from life. As we age, many of us begin to compromise. We give in to social or family pressures or biases (and sometimes, genuine needs): "You can't make a living as an artist; have something to fall back on," and so on. We slowly drift away from our highest purpose, and the clues start to seem meaningless. This book is about rediscovering the early passion and drive that you once felt as a youth, that once filled you with wonder and hope, and then applying the wisdom and strength of your older self to return to that early purpose and joy.

BREAKING IT DOWN: A PRAYER OF SURRENDER

As you learn more about yourself by practicing the exercises and answering the reflection questions in this book, you should begin to see similarities in every season of your life that gave you a sense of purpose. You should be able to see the kinds of activities that best fit your natural design. This takes having an open mind and surrendering yourself to self-discovery.

So get as comfortable as you can, say a little prayer, and surrender yourself to the present journey:

> *Dear Lord, I know You have a plan for me, and I believe You have been revealing it to me my entire life. Show me who I have always been to You. Reveal the virtues and gifts I did not know I possessed. Put me on a path to honoring the reason You made me.*
>
> *Amen.*

The Creator's Intent unlocks the opportunity to release the best parts of who you are. Your dream of being a fully realized Child of God comes awake when you are expressing the highest virtues of your spiritual self and living as a significant being in the world.

AT A GLANCE: LOOKING FOR THE CREATOR'S CLUES

1. Your past life holds important clues, and a self-assessment of your past journey is key to understanding your future potential.
2. Look for the preprogrammed aspects of your personality. They never change and should be honored and built upon. It is the truest picture of the Creator's Intent for your life.
3. Remember that you operate within God's bigger picture; your life is a piece of a larger continuum. It's important to keep that in mind while you are going through your individual issues.

4. How you respond to life situations, and life's many twists and turns, matters. Whether you model good or bad energy will be received and absorbed by those around you.

5. Patience is necessary. Discovery takes time, and rarely does someone just stumble across the Creator's Intent immediately. It takes the process of time and discovery to get to that point. Don't be in a rush.

6. Every event in your life is an opportunity. It's your decision as to whether any event, good or bad, can catapult you closer to a sense of purpose or hold you back. Trust that, in all things, a higher good is at work. Be patient and compassionate, and whether the event is a success or a difficult pain, Divine purpose will unveil itself.

7. Be intentional about noticing your clues. Set aside time to self-reflect. The answers are in the film of your past.

CHAPTER 7: CREATE ACCOUNTABILITY

"The most important quality I look for in a player is accountability. You've got to be accountable for who you are. It's too easy to blame things on someone else."

—Lenny Wilkens, former NBA head coach

Growing up in a relatively large family taught me a lot about the need for accountability. Having to answer to my parents and siblings for my actions trained me in the principles of accountability to myself and to the family pack, and these principles have stuck with me throughout my entire life journey.

Accountability to others challenged my ethics and helped me stand by decisions and answer for my actions. Even more so, having strong accountability has kept me on track to fulfill the greater purposes of my life. I refuse to live life or do business with people who have no one to challenge them or hold them responsible for their choices. You run the risk of being a casualty of poor decisions around a person who has no accountability.

When we first started the City of Hope International Church, there were just twelve of us in my living room praying, strategizing, and discussing how to move forward. I had so much fear in me that I was nervous as to what my next step should be. I had a vision and excitement, but I also knew that if people left jobs, moved across the country, or made decisions to financially contribute to this vision, then they would have certain expectations. Immediately, I knew that I needed to form a team of accountability partners who would hold me responsible for this new organization, so we created a committee board. But I realized that in order to be the compassionate leader I was designed to be, I needed accountability at a more intrusive level. I needed a group of people that I trusted who could really get in my business and challenge my heart as well as my actions.

The first such group of people I called were my spiritual leaders. These were men who had similar moral ethics to mine. Guys who wanted to protect me beyond my work; they wanted to protect my family, my role as a husband and father, my humility as a man in service to the community, and so on. These were family, long-time friends, and spiritual advisors who I allowed into my personal business. They were able to test my heart and ask tough questions to make sure my main priorities remained the focus of my life. And through these thorough and, at times, uncomfortable conversations, they helped me protect areas in my life I could not emotionally or spiritually afford to let fall apart.

The second group was comprised of high performers in my city—judges, businessmen, etc.—who just did it right. Men of wisdom, experience, and accomplishment. I am grateful I have always had access to such gems, because their accountability challenged me to maintain integrity in service. These guys could challenge why I was doing what I was doing. They made sure my motives were always pure and in service. I can still hear former US Magistrate Judge William McCurine reminding me, "Son, you can get rich for the purpose of serving, but you do not serve for the purpose of getting rich. I will not let you do that." He and others snap me back in line if I ever stray off purpose or become discouraged or battle weary.

Who keeps you accountable to your dreams? Who pushes you forward? Who challenges your integrity? Who can humble you if you get off course? This accountability is essential to protect the mission and the missionary.

PROTECT YOUR JOURNEY

God is the catalyst for transformation in your life. He wants to bring about positive change. Some of those changes will be radical: a new career, a new place to live, or the end of an old relationship. Others will be incremental, such as meeting new people or embarking on a fitness program. The scope of the changes doesn't matter; their effect does. God will only ask you to change as much as is needed to achieve His goals. Beyond that, any further change is your own decision.

Regardless of the scope of change, you've got to protect your journey to transformation, as well as the change itself. What does this mean? To protect the journey and the change means to make yourself immune to criticism and the doubts of others that could drive you off course. You must maintain your will and focus.

How did you arrive at the place where you decided to alter the course of your life? It matters. Whether it was something as simple as an epiphany birthed from reading a book or hearing a sermon, or something as painful as the lessons of loss and failure, the start of your journey matters. How do you protect the journey? One way is accountability, but another is by telling your story. Tell your stories; don't bury them. Share the truth about who you were compared to who you are today—and who you envision yourself becoming in the future! As you share the story, share it honestly. A sugarcoated truth is still a lie. Tell the truth about the players involved (even if you don't use names), how you felt, why you got there, and what you've left behind.

Telling the truth keeps the journey forever on your mind, reminding you of the paths you want to avoid as you progress. Also, protect your journey by validating your own experience, instead of waiting for others to validate it. It's fine to seek support and love from others, but remember that their own experiences, wounds, prejudices, and fears may compel them to see your journey as something far different from what you see. A good friend who has always been afraid to take a risk and live boldly might see his own failures in your journey and unwittingly undermine your confidence. Determine your journey's value for yourself, and you protect yourself from the opinions of others.

Don't let others' opinions determine how you should feel, how quickly you should heal, or who is of value in your new life. Your story is yours, you are where you are for a reason, and if you attempt to move forward from the platform of someone else's judgments, you will end in a place that fits their views, not your reality. Honor and protect your journey.

The changes that you are making in your beliefs, thoughts, and actions must also come under constant protection. The world hates a nail that sticks up; it will forever try to hammer it down. People who question the established way or defy conventional wisdom often face sanction and hardship. How do you protect your new mind-set and way of living from old habits and people from your past? How do you keep yourself from going back to the trash to retrieve your favorite shirt?

First, you secure yourself from "intention killers." As much as possible, you should eliminate from your life the things that tempt you back toward the old governing principles you once had: the people, places, counsel, and so on. Think of a recovering addict who avoids certain places, and the people who make going back to the addiction easy at all costs. Don't slack off on this. Be radical and aggressive. Your environment will determine whether or not the seeds of temptation grow.

This should be a priority for every individual who is striving to live life the way God intended! Again, take out your journal and make a list of anything that pulls you back toward the life that you've left behind, and do what you must to keep yourself protected from those things.

DON'T DO THIS ALONE

The other strategy that those seeking the Creator's Intent should adopt is to create a system of accountability:

> *You must make yourself accountable in order to achieve successful transformation.*

You are human, and like all humans, you are flawed. However, you also have the foresight to predict things that might happen and prepare for them. This enables you to take the single most important step in being successful in your transformation: finding people who will help you be accountable. There is no reason you need to go through this process alone. Ask for help.

Every serious person should have a person, team, or system that will hold them accountable for carrying out their commitments. This is about setting new, more demanding standards for yourself and then adhering to them whether you want to on a given day or not. When I was in the NFL I had a trainer, but I didn't need him to teach me how to do push-ups. I knew how to do push-ups! No, I needed the trainer to hold me accountable for *doing* them—to kick me in the backside when I needed it. People who understand your goals and values, and who will be intentional about holding you to them, are invaluable. They won't let you off the hook and will make you keep your promises, because your promises are always promises to *yourself.*

Even Jesus had a team of twelve guys who kept Him accountable to His task. King Solomon shared this wisdom, saying, "Two are better than one, because they have a good reward on their labor. For if they fall, one will lift up his companion . . . though one may be overpowered by another, two can withstand him" (Ecclesiastes 4:9–12). The principle of accountability works—if you let it. It won't do you any good if you have not experienced a profound desire to walk in God's purpose for your life. Furthermore, it doesn't help if you are unwilling to submit to the system or the partners you assign to holding you accountable.

Let's say, for instance, that part of your transformation is physical fitness, and you charge a friend with coming by your home three days at week at five thirty in the morning to work out. You tell her, "No matter how many excuses I make, get me out that door and running." But when she shows up, you resist and get angry. That doesn't work. However, when you submit to the truth that your accountability partner's sole purpose is to bring out the greatness in your life, helping you reach your God-assigned goals, then you are ready for the next level.

Mentors, coaches, books, and systems are useless if you are not willing to allow them to take a part in your life. To a healthy degree, you must allow them to be downright meddling, letting them mix into your life like milk in coffee. God will show you *what*, training will show you *how*, but it is up to your accountability system to ensure that you follow through.

The critical step in creating an accountability system is not scheduling, nor is it even choosing specific people. It's granting *permission*. You must give the people who will be holding you to the promises you've made to yourself and God permission to do so. You must clearly tell them that they are empowered to do whatever it takes to get you to stick to your plan, even if you're having a terrible day.

CREATE YOUR ACCOUNTABILITY PLAN

Let's take a look at four exercises that will help you stick to your accountability plan:

1. **Receive and state your intent to God and to yourself.** The two most important people you will ever enter into an agreement with are yourself and God. Between the two of you, your purpose can materialize. Through prayer, Scripture reading, life inspection, and the wisdom gained from mentors, you can grasp and understand the direction God intends for your life. You will definitely need experience, and maybe a counselor or mentor to help you decipher the specifics, but you can make sense of the Creator's broad intent on your own. Once you reach this place, state what you believe God intends for you and your intent to act by declaring: "God, I am clear that _____ and I intend to_____."

    Be clear. Be specific. There may be multiple commitments you have to adhere to, so write out more than one intention statement. It's okay to have three, or five, or ten.
2. **Create a plan.** The old adage "If you fail to plan, you plan to fail" is redundant, overused, played out, but also *true*. There's a difference between getting results and getting the results you want; getting any result is like intending to drive to New York but pulling onto any highway and going in any direction. The results you want don't

just happen; they are the outcome of intentional planning. Success is a system that needs to be created and deployed. If you want to complete what's in your heart and mind, start planning now. Put your ideas and plans down on paper and detail what you will do, when you will do it, how you will pay for it, whom you will do it with, what outcomes you are after, and so on.

When I wrote my first manuscript, I remember sitting with an editor with my well-collected writings neatly organized in a binder for her to simply edit. I thought she would be impressed with my content and presentation. After a few days of taking it all in, I called her to see how her work was coming along and what she thought. To my dismay, the conversation went something like this:

Me: "Hey, Nikki, have you had a chance to look at my book?"

Nikki: "Uh, yes, Pastor, I have."

Me: "Well, what did you think?"

Nikki: "Umm . . ."

Me: "Umm, what?"

Nikki: "Well, Terrell, tell me this, how much time did you spend on this?"

Me: "Oh, man, at least four months. Why'd you ask?"

Nikki: "Well, if I can be honest, what you gave me really isn't a book, it's just a bunch of collected writings. I mean, the stories are neat and interesting, but it doesn't have a flow or a real central purpose to it."

Me: "It doesn't? You don't think so?"

Nikki: "No, sir, not really. It was difficult to follow, actually. But I'm willing to help you with some direction if you need me to."

Me: "Uh, yes. I guess I do need some help. I'd appreciate that."

Nikki: "Okay, great. You can start by sending me your outline. From your outline I can take a look at your plan and get a better picture of what you were trying to accomplish."

Me: "Huh? Outline? Um, I, um, don't really have an outline, Nikki. I was just flowing as it came to me, you know?"

Nikki: "I see."

In seconds, my editor had gotten to the bottom of my problem and the reason for my unfocused thoughts: I had no master plan. A person can have great concepts and ideas, but with no plan to pull them together and give them direction, they meander and lose focus and end up meaning very little.

Look at your transformation plan like you're a baker. When a person bakes a cake, they start off with ingredients like butter, eggs, flour, and sugar. The plan to make all these elements work together is called a recipe, and it tells you not only the precise amounts of each ingredient to use but when to add them, how to add them, and how long to bake the final product. Without a recipe, the cook might end up with a gooey batch of warm paste. What is your recipe for bringing the Creator's Intent to fruition in your life? What I thought was a book was just a compilation of some writings that had no larger meaning to them. An outline—a recipe—would have made those random writings into a book.

With a plan, you can interweave events, activities, and talents into meaningful successes and finished goals.

Remember Proverbs 21:5: "The plans of the diligent lead surely to plenty."

3. **Set specific and measurable goals.** There's a wonderful saying that goes, "A goal is a dream with a plan." There are some coaches, pastors, and motivators who have gotten away from encouraging setting goals. I am not one of those people. Setting goals is how coaches get their teams to improve. It's how Jeremiah motivated his boss to allow him to rebuild Israel's city walls. It's how the prophets of old measured how far away the people had gotten from God. How will you know if you have achieved part of God's intention if you have no way to measure it?

    For instance, stating that you want to jog two miles in thirty minutes today is more specific and measurable than just saying "I want to jog two miles" or "I want to run for thirty minutes." Your goals should answer the who, what, when, where, and why of your expectation. Specificity will allow you to measure your performance—where you can do better, if the goal is too easy, too challenging, etc. This takes away the subjectivity of saying things like, "You did well." In whose opinion? Better to have measurable goals and *know* that you did well!

    Make your goals lofty enough to encourage your best effort and performance and get you out of your comfort zone, but reasonable enough that you can actually reach them. A Harvard Business School study performed by Ordóñez and Schweitzer in 2004 shows that people have a tendency to be dishonest with the outcome of their performance if they continuously fall short of their goals. We all feel self-conscious about failing, and that is the first step toward giving up. I don't want to encourage that, so set your goals at a level where you can achieve a measure of success. One step at a time.

4. **Choose your support team.** Having to answer to people is an amazingly powerful motivator. When you have to give someone a regular accounting of your progress and your dedication to your commitments, it becomes harder to backslide and slack off (which we're all tempted to do from time to time). If your intention is clear and your plans and goals are realistic, a great support team will be the key that unlocks your treasure. Pray, then handpick people who will demand your best and highest. Approach them with the utmost respect, and honor their journey, their attention to the will of God in their own lives, and their dedication to your well-being.

Set up regular meetings with your accountability partners and allow them into your space. Be honest about your achievements, failures, shortcomings, and frustrations. Remember, accountability teams are there for encouragement and to keep you true to your word. They will ask you the tough questions about your life and goals. However, though they may counsel you, they are not your counselors. They are not there to solve your personal problems. Get yourself out of your own jams and do not use their resources or contacts to help you do your assignment, unless that's offered. Instead, ask for advice, direction, principles, and wisdom. Prove that their advice is worth something to you by using it. Open your heart to their critiques as well.

A good accountability partner must have the room to "call you out" from time to time. Humbly submit to it if you're in the wrong and it will yield huge dividends. As Hall of Fame pro-basketball coach Lenny Wilkens says in his book *Have Fun, Try Hard, Play Fair*, "It's too easy to blame things on someone else." A good accountability team will help you make greater progress and keep you from bogging down.

BREAKING IT DOWN: PRACTICE CELEBRATING

A practice that I have recently started using in my personal life is that of celebrating and acknowledging every victory, large or small, and sharing that celebration with my accountability team. This runs counter to the way a lot of us treat ourselves—giving ourselves grudging credit for our wins while beating ourselves up for our letdowns. This is a failing model. Consider, instead, treating yourself to kindness and embracing the wisdom you gain when you fail. Plan some sort of celebration or acknowledgment when you reach even a small goal.

Compared to the finished product—the full realization of the Creator's Intent in your life—I understand that some victories seem tiny, and I don't encourage going over the top to celebrate. However, a goal accomplished is a goal accomplished. Take a moment and reward yourself and your team for the victory. Some things are as simple as recognition—a handshake, a gift card to say thank you, and so on. Others deserve more elaborate appreciations, such as a pay raise, a promotion, or a trip to a resort. Make it a point, particularly early in your new journey, to honor your achievements. Take a deep breath and pause to acknowledge the moment before you get back to the grind.

AT A GLANCE: CREATING ACCOUNTABILITY

1. The purpose of accountability is to protect you and your journey: to save what is important, to keep your mission focused, and to ensure the right motive.

2. Do not give the meaning of your journey over to a false interpreter. Others will be eager to define your journey based on their experiences. Don't move away from the meaning and tempo of your journey to satisfy someone's immediate need to fit you into theirs. Take your time. Heal fully. And honor what God is showing you.

3. The key to accountability is *permission*. You must grant permission to your accountability system to do its job if it is going to be effective.

4. Your victories, small or big, are worth celebrating and appreciating. Note your progress and wins. Do not take them for granted.

Chapter 8: The Turning Away

"If you want a happy ending, that depends, of course, on where you stop your story."

—Orson Welles

I was married to the love of my life, but after eight years, we got a divorce. I imagine I could write another book on why, but in the end—no blaming, finger pointing, or excuses—we just didn't work. It was the most unstable time of my life, and if you've ever lost a marriage you can understand the idea that marriage is a living thing. I hurt for me. I hurt for her. For my stepson. For our families and friends. For the people we tried to be an example for.

We are never so vulnerable to hurt than when we have chosen to love. Every night and day of the grieving process was painful. It left me feeling most dominantly like a failure, like a person who couldn't finish what he'd started and promised to do—a promise to a person but also to God. With each moment, I felt my confidence slipping away. While I never turned cynical toward life or God, or even toward her, I had lots of questions, epiphanies, aha moments, and realizations.

After our final decision was made to move on, one of the first promises I made to myself was that this would serve as a "comma" in my life and not a "period." There was more to my story. Operation Rehab My Life was underway.

NECESSARY ENDINGS

For new things to be born, other things have to die.

The fact that we are human, bound by limits that God has placed on our lives, motivates and inspires us. The fact of our mortality is one of the fundamental truths of our existence; we only have so much time before we must face our maker and answer for how we've served Him on Earth. That truth compels us to strive, explore, build, love, heal, create—basically, do all the things that have made human civilization possible. Without the fact of mortality hanging over our heads, we would very likely become unmotivated and indifferent about life. This is why people become more purposeful when they experience a life-threatening event or reach an age where they come face-to-face with their mortality. When you have all the time in the universe, what's another ten years of saying, "Well, maybe tomorrow I'll start writing that book"? But the threat of seasons ending and death produces focus.

Death is a force in creation. Beginnings lead to endings. But also, endings lead to new beginnings. The same is true for you as you walk this path toward the Creator's Intent and your own transformation. One of my other favorite Bible Scriptures says, "Most assuredly, I say to you, unless a grain of wheat falls into the ground and dies, it remains alone; but if it dies, it produces much grain" (John 12:24). I love it because, while it is spiritual in nature, it reflects a common and practical occurrence in our everyday experience. This is borne out in evolution, ecology, psychology, and even in the heart of the Christian faith itself: death produces life.

The mind of God is impossible for us to fully comprehend, but this much is clear: God intended for Jesus not only to be born as a man but to fully experience life as a man and to choose, based on what He saw in humankind, to take the sins of the human race upon Himself. Jesus may have been the Son of God, but He was also a man, with free will, capable of choosing to do otherwise. It was by His free choice to accept the burden of humanity's sins that He was then able to die and expunge those sins from the record, thus freeing all people and giving us a clear path to Heaven. Jesus followed a path that we all must follow as we transform:

1. Consciously choose to move forward into a transformative state.
2. Resist the urge to look back.
3. Accept that some things must perish so that we can fully enter into our destiny.
4. Accept these losses. There is no moving on without the loss of something that you will leave behind. An outdated part of you will die because you are discovering a new way to be you, and that's as it should be. As you begin to walk with God on the path of your mutual dream, you will have to accept some losses, such as:

   a) Your former career
   b) Relationships with certain people
   c) Old lifestyle habits
   d) The place you live
   e) Your personal, spiritual, social, and political worldviews

Once you make your choice to move forward and progress in the direction that God has always had in mind for you, some of these things will begin to die in your awareness. You'll begin to see less of people who should not belong in your life. You may feel out of place in a locale where you've lived for years. Your once-stimulating job may lose purpose for you. These are clear signs that it is time to turn away and not look back. Turning away from the dying parts of your past self is the essential act of commitment.

POSITIVES AND NEGATIVES

Progress is exciting and fun. In fact, progressing is like having a tailwind assist your purpose on its march forward. However, your past has potential to be an enemy to your progress. Your lifestyle, thought patterns, friendships and relationships, and your negative experiences can all lead you to believe things that are not true or to take actions that self-sabotage. At the same time, your past is also responsible for where you are today. It has been the river that has shaped the stone of your experience. Does turning away from your past mean forgetting all the lessons you learned and flushing your heritage down the drain?

No. It means striking a balance.

Too often, we subconsciously buy into the notion that the best indicator of our future is our past. Investment professionals often use this phrase to avoid making implied promises: "Past performance is no indicator of future results." For most people who are unrenewed thinkers, trapped in the patterns of their past like flies in amber, that's not the case. Past events are very much an indicator of what an unrenewed thinker will do. They are predictable, because they are not willing to pay the price of change.

However, you are a renewed thinker. Past is prologue for you, but not destiny. You have done the work of renewing your thinking, and you will put a team together to help you remain accountable to your new thinking and progress. When you have done that, your primary goal will be to answer this question:

Who or what do I have to turn away from in order to secure my dream?

The ideal spiritual life is one in which new ideas and effects are being born and old relationships and burdens are dying out in equal measure. This balance between death and life is essential and as old as the universe. There cannot be light and darkness together; one cancels the other out. You cannot hold on to the people, occupations, and habits you had in your past while at the same time walking in the footsteps of God to your ordained purpose! You must choose one or the other.

Over the years, you have adopted certain modes of thought and behaviors that simply don't serve you any longer. We all have. Well, it is impossible to continue in those thoughts and behaviors and experience the kind of radical transformation needed to walk wholly in your Creator's Intent. For example, if you discover that God's purpose for you is to aid the homeless, you can only embrace that purpose if you first free yourself from a longstanding belief that homeless people are all drug addicts who deserve to live on the street. That belief needs to die so a new one can be born.

You need to have a clear focus to achieve all that God has put in your spirit. As James 1:8 says, ". . . a double-minded man, unstable in all his ways." In other words, two or more polar thought patterns will compete in your mind for space until some are squeezed out. Unfortunately, too often the thoughts that are squeezed out are the ones you haven't practiced enforcing. That can leave old, nonproductive trains of thought—and the actions they provoke—to rule your mind. You can't produce from a place of abundance like that. Old thoughts have to die off in order for new ones to develop.

The story of Galileo from the seventeenth century is a perfect example of the necessity of releasing old patterns of thought before new ones can take hold. The Italian genius had used one of the first telescopes to discover not only the planet Jupiter and its moons but to find evidence that the sun, not the earth, was at the center of our system of planets. This angered the Catholic Church, which was holding desperately to the outdated dogma that the earth was the center of the universe. But because church officials were not ready to let go of this old belief, they persecuted Galileo, forced him to recant, and held him in captivity for the rest of his life. Actually, he got off easy: one of his contemporaries, Giordano Bruno, was burned at the stake for the same heresy.

It was only when the powers of that time finally let go of their outdated belief system that science and faith were able to collaborate to bring us many of the discoveries we have today. Until they were able to move on from old thinking, religious leaders could not get out of their own way.

That single idea will probably be the biggest challenge you face in moving onward in your journey. Most of us are deeply attached to our old ways of living. We want to be right. We like thinking that we've made good decisions in the past, and turning away from them can seem like a repudiation of our choices. But that's not necessarily true. Often, we simply evolve. We grow in understanding and wisdom and become able to see the signs God puts before us. Past choices and attitudes may have been right for the person you were ten years ago, but they may be obsolete today. That's why it is vital to move forward.

Paul the Apostle encourages this idea in 1 Corinthians 13:11: "When I was a child, I spoke as a child, I understood as a child, I thought as a child; but when I became a man, I put away childish things." In other words, a perfectly good apple can rot on the branch simply because it stayed there too long.

Sometimes, we are like that apple: we stay in situations well past their usefulness. This is how good things go bad, because we don't discern that it's time to transition to a new season. "Good-bye" is not always a bad word, but it is certainly a necessary one. That doesn't mean you have to burn up your old life. But you definitely have to limit its influence on your present.

MY TIPPING POINT

When I first started college, I didn't realize that, along with my bags and favorite blanket, I brought with me many of the attitudes, methods of surviving, and behavior patterns associated with being a teenager in St. Louis. I brought an edgy, dog-eat-dog mentality, and this sometimes led me to display aggressive, abrasive behaviors. It even caused me to choose and attract friends that had similar characteristics. They had different faces, but they were essentially clones of some of my old buddies from my neighborhood. During the latter part of my first year of college, I found myself the target of my resident advisor's anger.

One day, he overheard a few of my buddies and me joking around, playing loud music, and using foul language. Incensed, he burst in our dorm room and chastised us, saying, "This is an institution of higher education! What you guys are talking about, and how you guys are talking about it, makes you sound like you haven't left your old neighborhoods! If you want that life, then go back to that, but if you want what college can offer you, realize this opportunity and change how you approach this experience!"

Wow. That was a wake-up call. To this day, that resident advisor has no idea how profoundly that moment changed my life. It was a short, violent, angry rebuke, but in it he suggested that I had brought old ideas into a new season of my life, and they could not coexist with the journey I was currently on. His challenge made me review how I had approached this new opportunity, and I made the decision to detach myself from some of those old ways and embrace new ones—not only for survival in my new season, but also for the full development of my future.

My friends from St. Louis were and are amazing guys—they are some of the most brilliant people I've ever encountered, and many of them are doing very productive things—but the context of our experience growing up had produced a person who was different from the young man who was now attending college. That moment in my dorm room was a tipping point for me. I made the decision that, no matter how difficult it was, I was going to adopt a new philosophy for how I saw my college experience. My friends and I challenged ourselves to erase some of the negatives from our past and adopt new ways of thinking that better served our lives.

As I discovered through my college career, renewal is constant. You should have a regular practice, season after season, of sloughing off the skin of your past and taking on the reality of where you are today. Just the other day, I made yet another commitment to measure my salt and sugar intake. I have an extremely large sweet tooth, so making decisions to make better choices is a constant battle. Not long ago, I noticed that I needed to replace my candy consumption with a healthier choice. So I loaded my cupboards with fruit cups, yogurts, and snacked on quite a few health bars instead of candy bars. I noticed that my desire for eating traditional candies was curbed quite a bit, and I was pretty proud of myself. Then I found out that the new "healthy" foods I was eating had just as much processed sugar as the candy I had exchanged them for. I wasn't really changing; I was substituting. I have to constantly remind myself to check food labels as a part of my regular practice now. Change is difficult, but it is also necessary. Nothing is static in this world; even the mountains are being eroded as new mountains push up.

TRAIN FOR NEWNESS

Here are a few practical ways you can train your mind to adapt to new ideas that will help you develop in the newness of life:

1. **Determine what you believe.** Remember, you will speak what you believe, so pay close attention to your external and internal conversations. This way you can firmly know what you believe about yourself, your worthiness, your money and finances, your friendships and relationships, your faith, and more. This way, it won't be hearsay; it will be directly from your own mouth. Before you can determine *how* to transform, you must determine *what* to transform. Some parts of you and your life won't need to be left behind. Take some time, put those categories down on paper, and think about what you've been thinking and saying. Honesty is the key here.

    When I first did this exercise, I realized that in the area of finances, I had developed a belief statement that "just making it" was the ideal for financial health. I realized that as a child, that's all I had ever heard my parents say concerning money. We either didn't have enough or we were "just making it." I can still hear my father say to my mother, "Babe, we can't afford that." I didn't realize that these words set a ceiling on my expectations and governed the intensity with which I sought financial stability. Of course, I told everyone that one day I'd be wealthy, but deep inside, I didn't value saving, investing, or giving. Once I realized that this "false truth" was planted in my heart, I attacked it with all that I had. What false things have you adopted as your truth?

2. **Learn new ideas.** Replace negative ideas with a truth and a more helpful principle to guide your thinking. True transformation is no magic trick. If you are going to transform your beliefs, after you identify them, you are going to have to learn new ways to think. You will have to read or listen to books that will inspire and enlarge your mind. You'll need to listen to speakers and preachers who will encourage you with new wisdoms. Go to seminars and even work your way into a new community of people who will reinforce your new ideas.

    Financially, I knew that I had massive earning potential. I just didn't see past the false truth I was operating under with my "just making it" belief. I was in my own way because I never brought in new ideas to defeat the old ones. Things changed when I stopped speaking and reinforcing the false truth in my heart and started adopting new ideas. I read books, listened to financial leaders, attended seminars and webinars, searched the Holy Scriptures to get God's word on wealth, and even started conversations with people who saw wealth differently than I did. When I changed my belief, I changed my language—and *only then* was I really en route to transforming my life!

3. **Speak, speak, speak.** Attack your false truths with the same thing that planted them: words. Famed author Shad Helmstetter once said, "You can create the energy to turn your dreams into reality by knowing what to say when you talk to yourself." Well, what's your inner monologue now that you have identified your true beliefs? What will

you say to yourself and others now that you have new information to replace the old?

Part of your new habit of development and maturation should be saying new words and embracing new concepts that will serve you and refute your obsolete truths. Negative ideas can often seem to take up permanent residence in your mind and soul, so refute them by speaking aloud truths that serve you better! Some people say that speaking new ideas is hocus-pocus or a futile exercise, but they're wrong. Speaking it makes it real. It brings the ideas to life in your brain and your mind.

Notice how the words you speak habitually to yourself take root in your life and become your attitudes. I think you'll be shocked. We are what we say, and we have what we speak: "The tongue has the power of life and death" (Proverbs 18:21; NIV).

Use your words and language to uplift your psyche and encourage your being. Use it to do that for others as well. Speak well to your children, your friends, and to strangers. Start creating a language system that agrees with where your heart wants to go and the kind of person you want to become. For example, try saying:

- "I've got as good a shot as any person at that promotion."
- "I am not fearful of success because I've prepared myself for it."
- "I am a good person, well groomed, and fun to be around; if the object of my affection says no, it is based on his or her own judgment, not because I'm not desirable."

This is the type of conversation you *must* have to keep you healthy and ready to pursue your goals. You must be vigilant; old thoughts don't die easily. Be painfully positive. Be stubborn about the beliefs that you grant the power to govern your life. Even in the face of harsh realities, to transform your life, you must transform your language and mind.

Breaking It Down: Paying Attention

Actor Josh Hutcherson is quoted as saying the following about focus: "Life is like a camera. Focus on what's important and you will capture it perfectly." Everything cannot get your attention. There's a reason that we use the phrase "pay attention." It's because what we get in this life we buy with our attention. When God insists on leading you down a path, He is asking you to give it your full attention. We buy the life we desire with the attention we devote to it. This is why it is so important to be ever aware of the thoughts and actions from your past.

In our world, it's easy to let our attention become fragmented, splintered, and distracted. From TV news to the Internet to politics to mobile devices and entertainment, we live in a society that seems to be opposed to focus, reflection, and thought. A million flashing lights are constantly fighting for your attention—for your ability to be in the present moment and give your attention to what matters. The baggage from your past will do the same thing.

Attention matters because your attention will determine where your *intention* goes. Another great quote on focus is from the former prime minister of the United Kingdom, Winston Churchill: "You will never reach your destination if you stop and throw stones at every dog that barks." If you pay attention to those forces in your life that are aligned with God's intentions and the person you are becoming, your intentions will flow in that direction. You will receive what you pay for with your attention. If your attention goes to past unhealthy people or patterns of thinking, you will buy setbacks, resentments, and pain—none of which serve your new goals. Your attention and intention must be congruent if you are to achieve the results you want. You can intend to start a business and hire kids from the inner city to help them escape poverty, but if your attention is on the failed business ventures from your past, you will never get your new company off the ground.

Discipline your attention like you discipline your thoughts about the past. Refuse to place it where it can be wasted. Here are tips to help you pay attention and focus:

- **Prioritize what is important.** The most important things in your life should receive a premier position in your life. Write down a short list of your priorities and act accordingly. Prioritize your family and personal time, work time, rest and recreational time. Manage your life in such a way that the items at the top of your list get your present focus first.

- **Be careful of multitasking.** Sometimes multitasking is necessary. However, remember that the more things you have your attention on, the less bandwidth you will have for other important things you need to focus on. Multitasking makes you vulnerable to distractions. Whenever you can, do not take on more tasks that compromise your ability to offer each task pristine focus. Practice delegating or simply saying no.

- **Rest.** Proper rest and sleep give your brain a breather. If you're overworked or overloaded, your brain will pay the price. Sluggish performance and fuzzy focus are often the result of physical and emotional fatigue. So be mindful of what your mind needs in order to be sharp and able to concentrate through the completion of major tasks.

- **Pray.** Sometimes the things we worry about rob our focus. Personal worries cloud our focus and judgment. A solution is prayer. Casting the cares of your life onto the ever- strong shoulders of the Almighty get them out of your head and into His hands.

At a Glance: Turning Away

1. Some endings are necessary. The evolutionary process of death produces life. Some old books must be taken off your shelf to make room for new ones. Such is true with life. When a thing is taken off your life shelf, it is fitting to expect something new to replace it.

2. Don't allow thought patterns to stay too long or they will rot your thinking. Sometimes it's important to scrutinize what you think about and update your patterns.

3. New ideas must replace old ones. If you do not challenge your mind with new ideas, the old ones will creep back in and rule your thoughts again. Surround yourself with thoughts that reinforce your new thought patterns and ideas.

4. Move forward and honor your past. You can do both. Your past is responsible for where you are today and

should not be discounted or forgotten. Instead, honor and memorialize it, but move on from it.

5. Focus is key to achievement. Be careful giving your attention to things that are not a part of your ultimate goal. You cannot give everything your attention, so choose wisely and focus on aligning your attention with your intention.

Chapter 9: On to the Next Play

"He who moves not forward, goes backward."

—Johann Wolfgang von Goethe

In 1998, I remember playing against the Denver Broncos on prime time. The odds were against us as we were playing against the defending Super Bowl champions. We were an injury-depleted team playing for pride and a love of the game, going up against an all-star-studded opponent that was ending the year strong and making another Super Bowl push. Like most NFL games, this one was a fierce battle of back-and-forth competition. An intensely physical game with lots of big plays, trash talking, and gamesmanship—just the way I liked it.

Prime-time games tend to be the most exciting games for the fans and players because they are intentionally evenly matched, played at night, and usually the only NFL game airing, which means football lovers from all over the world are glued to a television watching. I was having a great game, running, catching, and using my versatility to make an impact for my team. It was a highly emotional contest as we were going toe-to-toe against the defending champions. I was taking it all in as the San Diego crowd was behind us, on the edge of their seats, responding to nearly every move either team made.

Sometime in the middle of the third quarter I ran a routine route, got past my defender, and was nearly all alone, but as the pass came to me, I turned my focus upfield before I secured the catch, and the result was that I dropped a pass that I should have easily hurled in. I could hear the crowd moan in displeasure as the ball hit the ground. Disappointed in myself, I jogged back to the huddle and sort of held my head down, shaking it from side to side in disbelief. While I was standing in the huddle waiting for the play to be called, I could hear my position coach from the sideline yelling, "Fletch!" *Oh Lord, he's mad,* I thought. Then again, "Fletch!" Noticing that I was trying to intentionally ignore him, he yelled again, but louder, *"Fletch!"* I could tell in his voice that I had better turn around for his next instructions or else be barked at, but instead, he looked at me intensely, with his index fingers pointing to his temples, and said, "On to the next play! On to the next play!"

His gesture was essentially saying, "Focus in, because the thing that's most important now is the next play." When life happens, for better or worse, your next decision is the most important one. Yesterday is gone. Today is happening. Tomorrow is the stage for your next battle. The reason you have to get over your past is because that battle is over— either you've won it or lost it. You've either done what you said or you weren't able to. There is no judgment or hard feelings about it anymore. There is nothing you can do to change its outcome, only its effects, so never allow anything to keep you in a battle you have declared is over.

I have spent a lot of time in this book challenging you to release yourself from the successes or failures of yesteryear. They can be debilitating and a hindrance if you gloat too long about a success or wallow too long in a failure. So our pasts are to be acknowledged, honored, and memorialized even, but ultimately let go of.

Today is where your current battle is. Right now, in real time, life is happening, and you can make choices that can shift the entire trajectory of your life. It may feel like a real battle, because for many of you, it is. But it is not without purpose. I hope with this book has helped to convince you of this fact. You are not out of the game; in fact, you are a decision away from being right back in the game—from turning the tables and operating in a life that honors you and the Creator's Intent. You are one pivot away from finding your congruence.

But no matter what did happen or will happen, the strategy for yesterday is over, the strategy for today is in play, but your tomorrow is what's in question. It's the only space in your life that is uninhabited and unaccounted for, and it is perfectly prepared for you to conquer it. Staying one step ahead is a key to winning any competition, and we cannot move on to the next level of your development without considering your next step: What is your strategy for tomorrow? What do you want it to look like in a year? In three to five years? In ten years? Is there a plan or vision for tomorrow? There had better be, because it's time to go on to the next play of your life:

The next play of your life should be carefully thought out, mapped out, and prayed over.

This book challenges you to discover your Creator's Intent, your life purpose, through embracing the journey of self-discovery. This answers the "why" of your life. However, that will not be all you will need for yourself—mission-focused goals are necessary as well.

What you will do and how you will fulfill your purpose is critical. How will you begin to move forward and what are you moving forward to? There will be quite a few ways you can choose to fulfill what you believe God has purposed you to perform. Deciding on which actions and when you will do them is important. Multitalented people, in particular, tend to want to perform each thing right away. To them my reminder is that you can indeed have everything God put in your heart, you just cannot have it all at the same time. Therefore, your patience, planning, and execution are important.

Many of us know that a goal is something to aim for, but few of us understand why that is important. The purpose of a goal is not to provide you with internal peace or joy. Goals are temporal. You can never demand an earthly virtue to supply you with eternal benefits. A goal is for here and now, energized by the things in the here and now. Faith, family, and meaningful relationships have eternal value. These are not goals per se; they are spiritual pursuits whose origin and fulfillment do not come from the earth but from the spirit realm.

Goals are not an end in themselves, which is why when you complete one, you desire to set another. Goals serve as expressions of and the stepping-stones to a much larger story being told about your life. The collection of pursuits, when in congruence with the Creator's Intent, will be telling the story of a larger purpose—the business, family, or the story of *you*. Your next play is to set appropriate goals that help tell a broader story.

For example, I am clear that I am to motivate, inspire, educate, and help every person I meet. Most every goal that I set—to build a church, start a school, have a family, be a mentor, be healthy—go toward that end. Are you thinking intentionally? Are you setting goals with the larger perspective of your purpose in mind, or are they arbitrary, without congruent meaning? When you set goals according to congruency there will be a heart connection that challenges you toward its fulfillment. To determine your potential goal congruency, ask yourself these five questions:

1. **Does this goal match your values and purpose?** Is this goal in alignment with what you know about yourself and who you know yourself to be? Will you have to be out of character to pursue your goal?
2. **Will this goal maximize your natural and spiritual competencies?** Will this goal utilize the virtues God endowed you with? Areas of our natural gifting lend to efficacy.

3. **Will this goal enhance, mature, or refine you in a way that brings value to the world when you're walking in congruence with God?** Some goals require skills and information that need to be learned: college, certifications, ongoing trainings, etc. These should be done in congruence with God, and not arbitrarily.

4. **Will this goal satisfy the need to express your virtues?** Remember that your virtues need an action to be expressed. Does the goal you have chosen provide that?

5. **Will the results of this goal help you get significantly closer to the meaning of your life story?** When accomplished, is this goal helping you tell the story of your life, or is it just an accomplishment that will be used merely for comparison with others?

"WHERE" IS AS IMPORTANT AS "WHAT"

Setting goals is an important next step, since your virtues need opportunities to express themselves. Remember, your virtues are core competencies and gifts that are preprogrammed in your DNA. You don't earn, borrow, or buy them. These are things you just have—God given. Over time you will or will not discipline, educate, or train these qualities, but you will desire to express them. Your virtues help you understand your usefulness on Earth and to God's great plan, so it benefits you to discover and train yourself in them as soon as possible. There is nothing more frustrating than yearning to outwardly express an inner gift and not knowing how.

The reward of operating in your virtues is a sense of significance, extreme joy and happiness, and knowing that you matter. However, each virtue must fit into an outlet that allows it to freely and regularly flow. This is the need for finding the right occupation—the where—to align your virtues. Some people pick jobs for the sole purpose of earning an income, and it is understandable and honorable to work so the needs of your family can be met.

However, a 2014 Gallup poll showed that on average, an adult full-time employee works forty-seven hours per week, almost a full workday longer than a standard nine-to-five. Shockingly, nearly four in ten of those workers said they work at least fifty hours a week! That's over nine hours a day for the average full-time employee. In a separate Gallop poll taken a year earlier, nearly two-thirds of all full-time employees said they were dissatisfied with their jobs. If the average employee sleeps eight hours a night, that leaves him/her with sixteen hours of usable time in a day. If that person works nine of those sixteen hours as the polls suggest, and fits in the category of the two-thirds of Americans who don't like their jobs, then he/she is dissatisfied for most of the day. In fact, over half of that person's usable hours would be spent feeling displeased.

What else do you imagine is affected by spending that much time of your usable day dissatisfied, unfulfilled, and frustrated? Your family life? Your physical and emotional health? Your time in worship? Your time to yourself? How you feel about yourself? Your recreational life? Feeling depleted will affect all of the above, and it will even interrupt those eight hours of sleep as well. But what if you found a place where you loved to work, because the work allowed you to express the best parts of you? Well, it's out there. The best part of my job is that it never feels like work. Literally, I get to motivate, educate, entertain, and inspire nearly every day of my life. My job is about so much more than inviting people into a relationship with Jesus Christ; it is also the place where my virtues are free to come out every day. I feel excited, significant, and fueled every time I take the stage to speak. Your occupation should be enjoyed, not endured. But many people just endure their jobs because they never find the place where their virtues best fit.

For me, where I do my job is as important as what I do. Being a court stenographer would bring me great stress. It's an honorable and necessary occupation, but it would not allow me to express my virtues. For starters, it involves minimal human interaction, virtually no speaking, no problem solving or impartation, and no structure for instruction. I would, however, encourage a person with my gifts and virtues to explore teaching, coaching, or even, yes, preaching. Because at each occupation, they would have the opportunity to showcase their virtues every day—a better fit than being a stenographer. Remember, it's not the job itself God needs expressed on Earth, it's your virtues. But it's your responsibility to find where your virtues can be best utilized and place them in a context where they fit.

RECIPROCITY

These days, part of my service to the community is to sit on a few local boards. Much of our role as board members is general oversight of the organization, ensuring its legal standing, protecting it, and in some cases promoting the vision of the organization. Consequently, in every board meeting there is a financial review portion on the agenda, when we evaluate how money is spent and allocated. Now, I have long known that I am driven by ideas and concepts and not numbers, so this portion of the meeting feels like God's punishment to me for every unseen thing I thought I'd gotten away with! It is almost physically painful to me to be in a board meeting during the financial review portion—thirty minutes feels like thirty hours when we're reviewing and comparing internal and external financial reports!

Okay, not literally, but I think it paints the picture of my disdain. It saps my energy. However, when the section of the meeting concerning next steps and vision updates comes up, I am like an eager kindergartener on the first day of school! Both portions of the meetings are noble acts that contribute to the whole; however, the difference is that one section is a better fit for my personal virtues. The result is that I am drained by one and energized by the other. This is called *reciprocity*—it happens when one's virtues and the right offering match up; two things are of mutual benefit to each other.

Have you ever found yourself getting lost and losing track of time doing something you love to do: playing ball, painting, singing, counseling, writing, cooking? Have you ever wondered why it seemed effortless, how you had the boundless energy to do it many times longer than anything else? The answer is reciprocity.

When you find congruence with the Creator's Intent, and you operate regularly in your virtues, the reward for your outflow is an equally and oftentimes greater inflow. One of the greatest promises of Scripture is found in Luke 6:38: "Give, and it will be given to you, good measure, pressed down, shaken together, and running over will be put into your bosom. For with the same measure that you use, it will be measured back to you." When you bless God with your willing congruence and expressions of your virtues:

He reciprocates by blessing you with an inflow of happiness, satisfaction, peace, strength to perform, and a sense of significance.

This is the reason why people who are operating according to their callings go to a job but never feel like they are at work. It is the reciprocation of Divine proportions being returned into their lives.

BREAKING IT DOWN: A PRAYER OF RECIPROCITY

Here is a prayer to acknowledge our Divine grace and gratitude for all that is past, present, and future. It's a prayer to demonstrate and

appreciate the interplay of all that comes and flows through the chan-
nels of God's reciprocity.

*Dear God, I give thanks for my life and the hope it receives
and the hope You use me to offer others. I only ask for the grace
to return to the world what You have so graciously sown to me.
I do not fret about my past, but I thank You for the lessons
hidden within it, and with anticipation, I look forward to
the unique ways You will make my successes, failures, hurts,
and places of wholeness honor You and others. I vow to You
and myself that I will pursue the goals and purpose of my life,
as You provide me with strength and inspiration. Today is a
great day to be me, and I am full of hope as I read the book of
my life, as You have already seen me.*

With my sincerest gratitude,

Amen.

AT A GLANCE: ON TO THE NEXT PLAY

1. No matter what happened, or will happen, the strategy
    for yesterday is over and the strategy for today is in prog-
    ress, but the strategy for tomorrow is in question. Are you
    prepared for your next move? Do you have a strategy?
2. Place your virtues in an environment where they fit, and
    give yourself the best opportunity to express them. When
    you find where you fit, it produces a sense of belonging,
    happiness, joy, and significance.

3. For those who honor God with congruence and the regular expression of their virtues, the Creator reciprocates with an equal and oftentimes greater return.

4. Goals are not an end in themselves; they merely serve as expressions and stepping-stones for a much larger story being told in your life. So do not look for the eternal values of joy, peace, and full contentment in your goals; they are only found in your purpose.

Final Thoughts: God's Cause and Effect

God did not intend your life to be a string of random events, haphazardly woven together, with you careening chaotically from one accident to another. Life can appear to be that way sometimes, but when you learn how to see the patterns and the underlying structure, you will notice that underneath everything is a Divine order—God's cause and effect.

Your life is not intended to be a reactionary event. When your life consists of reactions instead of proactive choices, you become like a prisoner with a warden who controls your comings and goings, highs and lows, joys and pains. You live life on your heels, constantly putting out fires, completely unable to anticipate the needs of tomorrow because every day is a crisis you are trying to survive. The crime that sends us to that prison? Not understanding the direction of your life.

Imagine walking on a forest trail that winds down a steep hillside. To stay on track, you must follow the many switchbacks as you zigzag across the face of the hill. Sometimes, the going is easy: you trot down smooth downhill stretches with little or no effort. Other times, the going is hard: you hit areas where the trail climbs or is blocked with rocks or brush, and the walk is sweaty, difficult, and even painful. But you must press on, and you must stay on the path. It may appear tempting to abandon the path and cut across the switchbacks, but this shortcut can make your journey harder, not easier. You might find yourself among jagged rocks, on a patch of ground suddenly too steep to descend or climb, or in a nest of rattlesnakes. No matter how arduous or tedious the trail may appear, staying on it is the only way to ensure that you will arrive at your destination.

Your life is that trail, and it was designed by God for you. His intention is that you should stay on the trail and, by confronting and overcoming obstacles and rough stretches, become stronger, wiser, and braver. Trusting the path God has laid out for you allows you to plan for what is to come in life. You can anticipate where the rough stretches will come and use your foresight to prepare for them—by inviting good people into your life or relocating to where the opportunities are, for example. If you leave the trail and decide to head into the wilderness on your own, who knows where you'll end up? Instead of preparing and bringing your wisdom to bear, you'll be reacting and living on the defensive. By the time you've realized that leaving the trail was a bad idea, you may be far from where God intended you to be, facing a long, discouraging hike back to your destined path.

I have seen it over and over again: well-intentioned people set out to walk on God's path and find the Creator's Intent. They say they are ready to leave their old favorite shirts behind and make a wholesale transformation to what they think and believe. They start off with fire and enthusiasm . . . and then, as time passes, they slip back into old habits. They call people who they intended to cut from their lives. They wander from the path and become lost again. It happens all the time. Sometimes, those who become lost never find their way back to the light.

Even if you know that God wants you to play a starring role in His plan, it is not easy to overthrow everything you've ever known in order to walk in His footsteps. It can be frightening. It can leave you feeling unmoored and adrift. That's where faith comes in. That's when you must consciously replace the belief that the unfamiliar is dangerous with the belief that, no matter what happens, God will not forsake you as long as you keep your end of the bargain.

Talk is cheap. Words mean nothing. Actions and intentions mean everything. A thing is worth exactly what you will pay to acquire it, and not a cent more. If you want something valuable, such as a new life, you must be prepared to pay and be responsible for it. No one said this would be easy. The journey to discover the Creator's Intent will be the adventure of a lifetime. It will be worthwhile.

A Note on the Significance of Prayer

In his book *Understanding the Purpose of Power and Prayer*, the late Dr. Myles Munroe calls prayer "the most important activity of humanity." Prayer is the dialogue between the Creator and His created, the place the created gains its guidance, pleads its case, and finds its refuge. Nearly every faith tradition requires prayer as an essential action for accessing power for purpose.

However, in the Christian faith, prayer is so prominent that we are admonished to "pray without ceasing," believing that our prayers serve as our permission for God to continuously intervene in our affairs. So far, this book has offered three simple prayers to use during your journey of self-discovery, and I have added them here again for your quick reference. And while you are doing the work, I encourage you to use these prayers, or create a variation of them, to invite the Almighty to assist you in this journey and to grow in His knowledge.

A prayer of faith (Chapter 4):

Father, I believe that You know all of the details concerning my life. I also believe that You want me to know them so I can live a life full of meaning and one that pleases You. Please share Your thoughts with me through events, associations, my history, and Your Word, so I can know who You see me to be.

Amen.

A prayer of surrender (Chapter 6):

Dear Lord, I know You have a plan for me, and I believe You have been revealing it to me my entire life. Show me who I have always been to You. Reveal the virtues and gifts I did not know about myself. Put me on a path to honoring the reason You made me.

Amen.

A prayer of reciprocity (Chapter 9):

Dear God, I give thanks for my life and the hope it receives and the hope You use me to offer others. I only ask for the grace to return to the world what You have so graciously sown to me. I do not fret about my past, but I thank You for the lessons hidden within it, and with anticipation, I look forward to the unique ways You will make my successes, failures, hurts, and places of wholeness honor You and others. I vow to You and myself that I will pursue the goals and purpose of my life, as You provide me with the strength and inspiration. Today is a great day to be me, and I am full of hope as I read the book of my life, as You have already seen me.

With my sincerest gratitude,

Amen.

One other important prayer that I am honored to write and leave with you is a prayer to accept Jesus Christ as your personal Lord and Savior. If you desire to receive Jesus as your Savior, simply believe and pray this prayer either aloud or in your heart:

Dear Jesus, I open the door of my heart that I may acknowledge my sins before You and ask for Your forgiveness. I believe that You are the Son of God who died on a cross for my sins. And I believe You rose from the dead and are alive today. I accept these as true and invite You into my heart to be my Savior. I receive Your forgiveness and the gift of eternal life with gratitude. Today I declare that You are my Lord. You are my Savior. And I am Your child. Lead me in a path that honors You and helps me fulfill Your purpose for my life.

In Jesus's name, Amen.

Appendix A:
Chapters at a Glance

The chapters at a glance from all nine chapters have been collected here for quick reference and access—perhaps pointing out a specific chapter or step you need to go back to and focus on. *The Book of You* can be carried with you throughout your life journey of self-discovery, and I hope you will come back to it as many times as you need to refresh and remind yourself, and rejoice in the knowledge that you are on a purposeful journey to your truest self—your Creator's Intent.

Chapter 1: Transformation Versus Change

1. Change and transformation are both useful and necessary. Change is less personally invasive, and the results are easily adjustable or even reversible. A life transformation, on the other hand, is extremely invasive—spiritually,

emotionally, and physically—and the results have a more permanent effect on your destiny and direction.

2. Transformation is an internal job, not an external one. Transforming your life begins in the mind and heart.

3. Transformation comes at a cost. This cost is the abandonment or total loss of many things and people, including your former self.

4. Transformations demand that you go all in. Your comfort zone will be disturbed. Transformation is about risking it all to discover the new you, the one your Creator intended.

Chapter 2: Finding Congruence

1. Our beliefs shape our limits. There are not many things that affect your ascension as profoundly as what you believe.

2. Congruence means finding your rhythm with God and His will for your life. A major key to discovering the Creator's Intent for your life is keeping up with the Divine pace of your life.

3. Beliefs control the thermostat of your life. How hard you pursue your passions will be determined by how much your core beliefs drive you to have them.

4. You cannot outrun your beliefs. Belief systems must be recognized, confronted, and then accepted or altered. You can move far away, but your beliefs come with you. Find out why you do what you do and prepare a plan to empower your new belief system.

5. Limiting beliefs can be reprogrammed. You are not doomed to a life of limitations. Beliefs can be adjusted to better serve the destiny of your life.

6. Success in the eyes of the world is a fleeting goal; you should redefine your goals around achieving personal significance and meaning.

CHAPTER 3: LEADING WITH YOUR PIVOT

1. Do not just make a change; make the *right* change.

2. Be responsible. A key dimension to moving to that pivot point and sticking with it is how we take responsibility for our past, present, and future decisions. It does not matter who is right or wrong; even if someone else did the damage, you must accept responsibility for who or what you've allowed into your life. Accept it, forgive yourself, and pivot.

3. You must participate in the events of your life in order for the Creator's Intent to be fully expressed in you. An unwilling participant will never reap the rewards of congruence. No burying your head in the sand. Get up and participate in your change!

4. If you have the capacity to make a poor choice, you have the ability to make a wise one; it's the same ability, just a different choice.

5. Own your faults. You will discover your dream only after you face the mistakes you've made in your past.

Chapter 4: Discovering Your Virtues and Calling

1. It's important to discover both your virtues and answer your calling.

2. Virtues are the most essential element to finding your Creator's Intent. They are the blueprint of your purpose.

3. You have expressed your virtues your entire life in some fashion or form. They come forth in every season, in everything, and share a common thread from childhood until now. Are you still operating in them or have you allowed life to get you off track?

4. A calling is the Divine beckoning of God to use your virtues. The weight of purpose will lead you to find ways to express your virtues to the world.

5. Your life has a natural bend toward inclinations and actions. Notice and honor them.

Chapter 5: Taking Off Your Favorite Shirt

1. Who you were can be an enemy to who you want to become. You do not have to abhor or dislike the person you were, only acknowledge that you must evolve into a wiser, more strategically congruent self.

2. Your past victories and failures can hold you back. Don't allow them to become the force that prevents you from moving forward.

3. The only thing that is at its absolute best in a comfort zone is comfort itself. You need challenges, and you need to participate in a space that stretches your gifts and intellect, which allows you to grow and produce beyond your dreams. Comfort zones don't build dreams; they maintain sleep.

4. God places the gifts that produce resources, opportunities, and the courage to seize them on the pathway toward your purpose. If you follow where God is calling, these things are sure to appear.

5. Faith is the currency of the extraordinary. Spiritual resources require faith. Faith in yourself, but also faith in the Divine realm, is often overlooked and underutilized. Do not think it strange to summon Heaven for supernatural intervention. And think it even less strange to expect it. It's okay: ask God for it.

6. Bondage requires you carry a burden; freedom requires you carry responsibility. The trade-off to being in control of your life is that you will now be the sole person responsible for it. No one will tell you what to do, but how you envision discipline, effort, research, and fortitude matter. You can forfeit this and be a worker in someone else's vision, or you can carry the weight of responsibility and live out the vision God gave you.

7. "Beds are made; decisions are lived with." Make your decision and prepare to live with the results.

Chapter 6: Looking for the Creator's Clues

1. Your past life holds important clues, and a self-assessment of your past journey is key to understanding your future potential.
2. Look for the preprogrammed aspects of your personality. They never change and should be honored and built upon. It is the truest picture of the Creator's Intent for your life.
3. Remember that you operate within God's bigger picture; your life is a piece of a larger continuum. It's important to keep that in mind while you are going through your individual issues.
4. How you respond to life situations, and life's many twists and turns, matters. Whether you model good or bad energy will be received and absorbed by those around you.
5. Patience is necessary. Discovery takes time, and rarely does someone just stumble across the Creator's Intent immediately. It takes the process of time and discovery to get to that point. Don't be in a rush.
6. Every event in your life is an opportunity. It's your decision as to whether any event, good or bad, can catapult you closer to a sense of purpose or hold you back. Trust that, in all things, a higher good is at work. Be patient and compassionate, and whether the event is a success or a difficult pain, Divine purpose will unveil itself.
7. Be intentional about noticing your clues. Set aside time to self-reflect. The answers are in the film of your past.

CHAPTER 7: CREATING ACCOUNTABILITY

1.   The purpose of accountability is to protect you and your journey: to save what is important, to keep your mission focused, and to ensure the right motive.

2.   Do not give the meaning of your journey over to a false interpreter. Others will be eager to define your journey based on their experiences. Don't move away from the meaning and tempo of your journey to satisfy someone's immediate need to fit you into theirs. Take your time. Heal fully. And honor what God is showing you.

3.   The key to accountability is *permission*. You must grant permission to your accountability system to do its job if it is going to be effective.

4.   Your victories, small or big, are worth celebrating and appreciating. Note your progress and wins. Do not take them for granted.

CHAPTER 8: TURNING AWAY

1.   Some endings are necessary. The evolutionary process of death produces life. Some old books must be taken off your shelf to make room for new ones. Such is true with life. When a thing is taken off your life shelf, it is fitting to expect something new to replace it.

2.   Don't allow thought patterns to stay too long or they will rot your thinking. Sometimes it's important to scrutinize what you think about and update your patterns.

3.   New ideas must replace old ones. If you do not challenge your

mind with new ideas, the old ones will creep back in and rule your thoughts again. Surround yourself with thoughts that reinforce your new thought patterns and ideas.

4. Move forward and honor your past. You can do both. Your past is responsible for where you are today and should not be discounted or forgotten. Instead, honor and memorialize it, but move on from it.

5. Focus is key to achievement. Be careful giving your attention to things that are not a part of your ultimate goal. You cannot give everything your attention, so choose wisely and focus on aligning your attention with your intention.

CHAPTER 9: ON TO THE NEXT PLAY

1. No matter what happened, or will happen, the strategy for yesterday is over and the strategy for today is in progress, but the strategy for tomorrow is in question. Are you prepared for your next move? Do you have a strategy?

2. Place your virtues in an environment where they fit, and give yourself the best opportunity to express them. When you find where you fit, it produces a sense of belonging, happiness, joy, and significance.

3. For those who honor God with congruence and the regular expression of their virtues, the Creator reciprocates with an equal and oftentimes greater return.

4. Goals are not an end in themselves; they merely serve as expressions and stepping-stones for a much larger story being told in your life. So do not look for the eternal values of joy, peace, and full contentment in your goals; they are only found in your purpose.

APPENDIX B:
GLOSSARY

Here is a glossary listing many of the key spiritual principles and definitions *The Book of You* teaches, for easy reference and as a gentle reminder at any point in your journey.

On Creator's Intent:

God's conceptual purpose and possibility for your life that includes your highest intended functions that ensure accompanying results.

The Creator had (and has) a specific, purposeful intention for how you should be using your life and your gifts.

If you are to know it, you must pursue the Creator's Intent and live according to it.

On Transformation:

What brings you into alignment with the Creator's Intent may change depending on the life stage you are in.

On Congruence:

The place where your life is in harmony with God's rhythm.

On Belief:

God believes in you even if you don't believe in Him.

What you have been conditioned to believe will determine what you permit yourself to achieve.

On Pivot:

The right change in how we think or act today can change all the outcomes of tomorrow.

On Responsibility:

You are responsible for who and what you let into your life and how much power you grant them over you.

On Virtue:

God places the DNA of your purpose in your personal virtues.

On Calling:

Your calling is simply the pull from God on your heart and conscience for you to express your virtues consistently to the benefit of yourself and others.

On Free Choice:

God lays down the path that you should walk; life itself brings obstacles, but you must decide how you will respond to the obstacles if they are to be opportunities.

On Creator's Clues:

God is working in your life to guide you to who you were meant to be.

On Accountability:

You must make yourself accountable in order to achieve successful transformation.

On Turning Away:

For new things to be born, other things have to die.

Who or what do I have to turn away from in order to secure my dream?

On Next Play:

The next play of your life should be carefully thought out, mapped out, and prayed over.

On Reciprocity:

God reciprocates by blessing you with an inflow of happiness, satisfaction, peace, strength to perform, and a sense of significance.

Acknowledgments

These types of projects cannot be done in isolation, so a tremendous thanks is in order to many people, but namely: my parents, Hosea and Edna Fletcher, and my siblings—Myron, Tracy, Bryan, and Shaun— you all encouraged me past my limits in this season and challenged me not to give up. You held up my arms while I was in the fight of my life. I love you all and am honored to share your name. We will all do even greater things while we are on this Earth!

Trey, the "bonus" who remains. You'll probably never know how loved you are, how inspiring you are, and how your presence brought such meaning. You're a real "Ace." Love you beyond life, kid. #NeverAStepAlwaysABonus.

The reality is that my friends are better than yours: to the host of you, old and new, you inspire me to run like the wind. I appreciate you all beyond reason because you let me be me, and you still love me. Love ya'll back.

To the City of Hope International Church family, for their unrelenting faith in what God is doing in my life. We are a tribe that wars on forever, governed by our Savior, manipulated by no one, and authentic to our core. Wherever life takes us, I journey with you because "I am the City."

To two very special people who are no longer with us:

Brian Klemmer, who was the first person who told me that my story was worth telling. You gave tools, inspiration, and challenges to thousands of us, and even though I knew that I wasn't the only person you made those early personal inspirational calls to and gave free books to, you made me feel like I was. I want to inspire like you.

And to Cory Hampton. You simply were the best friend I've ever had. Hope they let you read other books in Heaven besides the obvious one! Miss you, man!

The Ascendant Group and Sophia Nelson: When Sophia introduced me to you guys, she told me to put on my seat belt, and she was right; you guys worked so hard and so fast that my head was spinning. Thanks to Sophia and the Ascendant team for believing in me and not letting this journey be wasted.

My G-VI crew! Big dreamers do big things, right? Well, I'm just getting started. You all inspire me so much. What we do and hold one another accountable for is destiny to go to another level.

Finally, to my Savior, Jesus Christ: lover of my soul, keeper of my secrets, holder of my future. You are the One who sees all and never leaves. Thank You for trusting me with the message of hope. I pray the world hears Your voice through me and heals. Thank you, Abba Father.

About the Author

Ordained pastor Terrell Fletcher is a former NFL running back and elite Big Ten Conference rusher turned global visionary, provocative thinker, and author. He serves as senior pastor of the City of Hope International Church, a multicultural, faith-based, global humanitarian organization based in San Diego. He has a distinct love for motivating young emerging thinkers, professional athletes, and community influencers. As a global speaker, he seeks not only to inspire but also to deliver practical tools for sustained empowerment. He has shared his message of transformation and hope in many parts of the world, including Nigeria, Côte d'Ivoire, Uganda, and Belize.

Fletcher lives in San Diego and serves as the chaplain for the San Diego Chargers football organization. He is also an active alumnus of the University of Wisconsin. Fletcher holds a bachelor's degree in English literature and a master's degree in religious studies. Follow him on Twitter @terrellfletcher, or visit www.terrellfletcher.com for more about the author and his work.